Elevate Your Excellence

Elevate Your Excellence

The Mindset and Methods that Make Champions

Christina Heilman

MOMENTUM PRESS HEALTH

MOMENTUM PRESS, LLC, NEW YORK

Elevate Your Excellence: The Mindset and Methods that Make Champions

Copyright © Momentum Press, LLC, 2017.

First published in 2017 by
Momentum Press, LLC
222 East 46th Street, New York, NY 10017
www.momentumpress.net

ISBN-13: 978-1-94474-949-1 (paperback)
ISBN-13: 978-1-94474-950-7 (e-book)

Momentum Press Health, Wellness, and Exercise Science Collection

Cover and interior design by Exeter Premedia Services Private Ltd., Chennai, India

First edition: 2017

10 9 8 7 6 5 4 3 2 1

Printed in the United States of America.

*To my family who have helped me to be resilient
in the face of struggles and successes.*

*"Yesterday I was clever, so I wanted to change the world. Today I am
wise, so I am changing myself."*

—Rumi

Abstract

Elevate Your Excellence: The Mindset and Methods that Make Champions is a peer-reviewed sport psychology text designed to help individuals find new ways to enhance mental functioning that optimizes performance and health. Whether you are an athlete, coach, exerciser, or just looking for ways to excel in another walk of life, this book covers the core components of the mental game to skyrocket performance and personal excellence.

With current research, science-based skills, and expert advice, discover how to:

- Develop optimal levels of motivation.
- Set effective goals to reach your potential.
- Manage emotional and mental fluctuations to peak under pressure.
- Strengthen imagery ability to achieve excellence.
- Maintain a more positive outlook to ward off limiting beliefs, overcome slumps, cope with injuries, and deal with other obstacles that may hinder your success.

Each chapter covers the concepts, theories, and research behind each mental skill. The mental skills include: myths of mental training, motivation, goal setting, energy management, peaking under pressure, and imagery. After learning about each mental skill, specific, real-world strategies are provided to improve your mental game as well as how to appropriately implement these mental tools and tactics into training, competition, and life.

Both practical and palatable, *Elevate Your Excellence: The Mindset and Methods that Make Champions* is an essential part of your training arsenal to reach your potential and beyond.

Keywords

athlete, coaching education, goal setting, health, imagery, mental training, mindset, motivation, performance anxiety, performance excellence, sport performance, sport psychology

Contents

Acknowledgments

Thanks to Abby Larson, Eric Carlson, Sam Elias, and Brian McDermott for the various degrees of editing and input. I truly appreciate each one of your efforts and insights.

Introduction

Many champion athletes recognize that sport is played with the body, but won in the mind. Most athletes who are at the top of their game have skillfully learned how to manage their energy, focus, motivation, and anxiety under pressure. Along with training their bodies, champion athletes have also spent hours training their brains to find strategies that help them consistently play at their peak.

Hence, it's a fallacy to believe champions are born and not made. Staying focused despite distractions, keeping calm under pressure, letting go of self-defeating thoughts, and maintaining a positive perspective after making a mistake are not innate or instinctive. Rather, developing awareness around the mind's limiting tendencies and gaining healthy tools to manage mental fluctuations improves our ability to play to our potential. Thus, winning the mind game and performing optimally is a result of consistent, systematic mental training and not from some innate quality that an athlete is born with. Each of us has the capability to strengthen our mind and body to reach peak levels of performance, health, and enjoyment in sports and life.

This text is designed to educate athletes, coaches, exercisers, parents, and practitioners with the foundational mental skills, science, and strategies to achieve an ideal combination of performance and health. The beginning of each chapter is meant to inform the reader with the concepts, theories, and research behind each mental skill. Next, the reader will gain straightforward strategies to develop a strong mental skill set and implement those positive skills, habits, and attitudes into their own life or to guide athletes in better understanding how to optimize their mindset. The hope of this text is that readers learn the best science, skills, and inner strengths to skyrocket their success in sports or in any area of life.

The formula of the mindset and methods of a champion is simple: *by applying yourself at becoming a little better every day, over time you become a lot better.* With consistent practice, you will start to see the small changes pay off and excellence begins to cascade in all areas of performance—sports, school, work, wellness, and so on.

The first step in achieving a stronger mindset is making the choice to dive in and get started. Owning this book is a good start. Congrats! The next step is about having the commitment and consistency to continually make it happen. It will take passion and persistence on your part to read, reflect, experiment, adjust, practice, and master. To accomplish this, I suggest reading one chapter at the beginning of the week and practice the new tools and tactics for the remainder of the week. By the end of six weeks, you'll have a solid foundation in training your brain for excellence. If you have any questions, please don't hesitate to reach out at chris@mindset-coach.com.

CHAPTER 1

Introduction to Mental Skills Training

"Baseball is 90% mental; the other half is physical."

—Yogi Berra

Yogi Berra's numbers don't add up, but his advice is well taken. Physical skills and conditioning are traditionally a major focus of a successful athlete's daily regimen, but psychological factors such as confidence, concentration, and emotional regulation also play a significant role in achieving peak performance, 90 percent according to Berra. What are your thoughts on this topic? How much of your sport, career, or life is made up of mental versus physical training? Another way to put this is "What proportion of sports performance is attributed to mental factors and what proportion is due to physical factors?"

_____% mental

_____% physical

In asking hundreds of athletes, coaches, trainers, and medical staff this same question, most reply that 50 to 90 percent of their game is mental (Heilman, 2017). Yet, when asked if they work on the psychological aspects of sport, most indicate they spend little to no time devoted to these important skill sets. That doesn't make sense!

Often times athletes, coaches, or athletic trainers shy away from mental training because they simply don't have the knowledge or tools to aid in psychological skill development. This book is intended to help athletes and practitioners better understand the mind's limiting tendencies as well as how to develop positive mental habits and attitudes that facilitate reaching higher levels of human performance and health.

In my experience, many athletes neglect working on their mental game because they view it as a sign of weakness, being soft, or fearing that they might be labeled as a head case. In reality, mental training is for those who want to *achieve amazing feats of physical and mental performance* and attain personal peak performance, be it in sport, wellness, career, or interpersonal relationships.

What Is Mental Skills Training?

Initially, it is important to understand the meaning of *mental skills training (MST)* and how it can be a beneficial tool for achieving performance and personal excellence. MST can be best understood within the context of sport psychology. First, let's tackle the term psychology. *Psychology* is a product of your mental functions plus your behaviors.

- *Mental functions* are an individual's perceptions and how the brain processes thoughts, feelings, and environmental conditions.
- *Behaviors* are our actions or how we react to our mental processes.

As an example to explain the term psychology, think back to a past coach or teacher who had a positive impact on you. Imagine for a moment that this coach or teacher looks irritable and is frowning at you. What is your reaction? Do you automatically think your coach is mad or frustrated? Do you assume that your coach might be upset with you? If so, how do you decide to approach your coach? Do you choose Option A: stay far, far away; or do you go with Option B: approach coach and ask, "What's going on?"

It's likely that if you selected Option A, you viewed your coach's frowning face as being angry and not approachable because of the fear of his or her possible reaction toward you (i.e., "maybe coach is mad at me and is going to yell at me…"). However, it is also possible that your coach ate a bean burrito for lunch, which caused an upset stomach thereby causing the irritable face! But since you never communicated with your coach, this actuality remained unknown.

This example is meant to point out that *psychology is based on our perceptions of the situation*. Based on our perceptions, we decide to either take a step forward or take a step back. Our perception is what propels us to take action and attain greatness or it is the very thing that holds us back from achieving the things we want most.

Abraham Maslow (1970), an American psychologist in the 1900s, studied the greats of his era–like Albert Einstein and Eleanor Roosevelt– and what he learned is that in any given moment we have a choice. A choice to step forward into growth or a choice to step back into safety. Philosopher and entrepreneur, Brian Johnson (2017), explains the concept of stepping forward or stepping backward in terms of +1 or –1. Moment-to-moment-to-moment, we have a choice, +1 or –1. Meaning, in each moment we can choose to either step forward (+1) or step backward (–1). At the end of the day, these micro-decisions bring you closer to being a champion and living a life you love or they take you further away. And what happens when you compound these daily micro-decisions into weeks, months, and years? Voila! That's your life. That's how you actualize your potential or not. Psychology, simply put, is what happens between the ears (mental functioning) and what we *choose* to do about it (behaviors).

Now, let's discuss *sports*. What is unique about sports? Sport is an arena to voluntarily push our limits–to see what we're made of. It's an avenue to connect to a like-minded community, set goals, and pursue dreams. Pursuing dreams gives us meaning, purpose, and joy and provides us with the power to persist through the ups and downs. Sport also challenges us to preserve and maintain perspective within our personal pursuit of excellence...step by step, day by day. Ultimately, sport is an avenue to keep us strong in mind and body and soul.

Sport psychology, then, is the scientific study, within the context of sport, of how the brain processes experiences and emotions such as anxiety or confidence and how you react to those experiences (i.e., take a step forward or step backward). As an example of these experiences and your reactions to them, imagine a time when you were about to start a competition. Do you remember feeling butterflies in your stomach or your heart racing? How about an increase in the acuity of your senses or even cat-like focus? Did you perceive these emotions as a sign of excitement or nervousness? Depending on how the brain processes bodily sensations and emotions, pre-competition arousal can either allow one to confidently perform or cause one to choke under pressure. In essence, sport psychology is about YOUR perspective of your sporting environment, abilities, limitations, and potential as well as how you process and react to these perspectives.

Sport psychology uses MST as a means to change negative perceptions and emotions into something more positive. As Maslow (1970) said, "If you deliberately plan on being less than you are capable of being, then I warn you that you'll be unhappy for the rest of your life." Consequently, MST can allow an athlete to perceive challenging situations as an opportunity to grow, improve his or her self-confidence, reframe negative self-talk, and live a happy, healthy life. MST is meant to develop a strong mindset of focus, discipline, passion, commitment, strength, and fun. MST can also improve the ability to stay focused in the present moment so mental and physical strengths and skills can be optimized. Thus, MST is about experiencing excellence. The core MST components include: *motivation, goal setting, arousal control and stress management, imagery, and self-confidence.*

MST is much like physical conditioning. An athlete doesn't lift weights for one day and think: "I'm good. I'm strong. I'm ready to go." We know that a one-time weight training session doesn't improve muscle strength or size. Similar to weight training, in order to grow, improve, and succeed, mental conditioning requires consistent effort and must be viewed as a long-term part of the overall training program. Weinberg and Gould (2014), sport psychology researchers and practitioners, define MST as *the systematic and consistent practice of developing psychological skills for the purpose of enhancing performance and promoting positive experiences in sports. Systematic* practice means that mental training is not a magic pill, a one shot deal, or a single team building session at the start of the season. Therefore, the goal of this text is to teach a skill-oriented, systematic approach to MST as a means to improve both sports performance and personal excellence.

An example of adventure racers using sport as a way to voluntarily push their limits, pursue a dream, and overcome obstacles to achieve greater personal and performance satisfaction

Why Mental Skills Training?

All athletes fall victim to mistakes, slumps, and doubts. But the most successful athletes have the mental skill set needed to face challenges and maintain the motivation and focus that is necessary to push beyond the hard times and achieve high levels of excellence. There's evidence to support that the most successful athletes spend more time mentally preparing for training and competitions and do so more consistently compared to their less successful peers (Greenleaf, Gould & Dieffenbach, 2001; Krane & Williams, 2006). Great athletes have a superb ability to cope with stress, manage emotions, set challenging (yet realistic) goals as well as visualize and achieve success (Krane & Williams, 2006, Weinberg & Gould, 2014). The best athletes have more than just elite physical skills, they also have elite psychological skills and often it's those skills that separate the good from the great.

MST can improve sport performance but these skills can also be used to improve performance in many of life's challenges. Mental training helps to strengthen your brain to focus better, be more resilient in the face of adversity, and build the confidence needed to pursue challenging goals. The strategies used to confidently perform your best in sports are especially valuable because these skills can also provide you with the ability to excel in and enjoy all aspects of life, including school, career, and interpersonal relationships. Therefore, *anyone* can benefit from MST! Naturalist and biologist, Charles Darwin, puts it this way, "It's not the strongest or the most intelligent who will survive, but those who can best manage change."

Myths About Mental Skills Training

If MST is an important aspect in managing change, boosting performance, and promoting enjoyment in sports, why is it often *not* part of regular training? There are many reasons why MST is dismissed, neglected, or overlooked. The three main myths of mental training include: (1) there's not enough time, (2) it's only for those who have deep psychological issues, and (3) it's a quick fix that will immediately improve sport performance (and when it doesn't, practice of MST is often abandoned).

Myth 1: Not Enough Time

There's no doubt that mental training takes time. However, taking as little as 5-minutes prior to practice or training to focus on breathing and centering oneself can be a time-effective and simple way to start integrating mental skills into a daily training regime. This time also serves to set the stage to enhance the quality and enjoyment of the upcoming training session and set aside distracting thoughts and troubles. Small, consistent mental training efforts can make a big difference in mindset and performance. My client, professional rock climber, Joe Kinder, practiced some of the mental skills outlined in this text. This is what he had to say:

> I was skeptical as to how a sports psychologist would help in my climbing life as I thought I was pretty balanced out. Over multiple days and conversations with Chris I have now implemented many small practices that have changed my climbing life and life in general.

If you are skeptical of mental training, I encourage you to try it for yourself. Take the next couple minutes to imagine how you want the rest of your day to go. To guide you through this exercise, follow the imagery script as shown next:

Mental Exercise: Imagine How You Want Your Day to Flow

Begin by sitting comfortably on a chair. With good posture, close your eyes and take five deep, relaxing breaths. Don't try to change your breathing. Simply focus on the in-breath and out-breath. For a few breaths, notice how the rhythm is naturally calming and peaceful. Next, imagine how you want your day to unfold. Start by how you plan to transition from this short imagery script into how you want to read the rest of this chapter. Do you want your reading experience to enrich your life or is reading this book a task you simply need to check off the list? Next, begin to visualize how the rest of your day will flow. How will you manage your day in a way that best supports you? What excites you? How can you embrace that excitement? Also, what are the foreseen obstacles or challenges that you may encounter? Can you imagine yourself overcoming these challenges? Can you think of a word or image, such as *flow, streamline,* or a *stable mountain,* that describes how you want your day to unfold? Next, imagine how you want your evening to play out? What things are part of your bedtime routine that help you to sleep soundly? With three more refreshing breaths, softly open your eyes. Resume your casual posture and enjoy the reading experience.

Tonight, as you lay your head on your pillow, take a moment to reflect on this imagery. Did it make an impact on how your day went?

As a final point for the athletes and coaches who feel they barely have enough time to develop physical skills, techniques, and tactics, and can't imagine finding the time to include MST: take a moment to reflect on a particular poor performance. Common reasons for poor performances often include: "I just couldn't focus," "I freaked out," or "I was too tense and tight and had trouble getting into the zone." If mental mistakes are often to blame for a poor performance or a lost game, then why are athletes and coaches not taking the time to refine concentration, confidence, and courage to go beyond what they think they are capable of doing? Take the sentiment from Prussian philosopher Wilhelm von Humboldt, "True enjoyment comes from activity of the mind and exercise of the body; the two are ever united." Wouldn't you agree that synergy of the mind and body is when we perform our best? Because the mind is our most powerful asset, for optimal mental and physical performance, it is also essential that we spend at least a few minutes every day to strengthen and refine our mental performance.

An ultrarunner and working mom using mobility and mental training exercises as part of her daily training program to balance health and boost performance

Myth 2: Mental Training Is Only for the Depressed, Anxious, and Angry

It easy to believe that MST is only for *problem* athletes who suffer from psychological issues.

Often athletes and coaches believe that only individuals with eating disorders, severe depression, or deep-rooted psychological issues see a sport psychology *shrink*. In reality, only about 15 to 33 percent of collegiate athletes experience mental disorders that require a clinical psychologist

(Solomon, 2016). However, because of the stigma surrounding psychology, the other 67 to 85 percent of athletes might be hesitant to work with a sport psychology coach. In reality, many elite athletes like Kobe Bryant, Russel Wilson, and Carli Lloyd don't have clinical psychological issues, but work with a sport psychology coach to improve their mental game.

Myth 3: MST Is a Quick Fix

It's typical for parents and coaches to contact me the week before a *big* competition and ask me to mentally prepare their children or athletes for the championship game. The days before a competition are not the best time to work on one's mental game. The best time to start MST is in the pre-season or off-season. Why? Honing one's psychological skills takes time. It requires deliberate practice just as physical training does. In the few days before a championship game, it's unlikely you would try to learn a new physical skill or trick and use it in competition because you haven't put in the time to master the skill. The same concept applies to mental training. The new mental skill hasn't been mastered so it's not a trustworthy tool to use in competition.

Although consistent practice is necessary, the good news is learning a new psychological skill is not a huge time commitment. In general terms, practice begins in a safe setting (e.g., bedroom, locker room) for five to 30 minutes, three to five times per week. After practicing a mental skill in a safe setting and becoming proficient at using it, the next step is to practice the skill in training and then bring it to competition.

Once an athlete learns a mental tool and becomes skilled in its use, less time is needed to practice. It is similar to learning how to ride a bike. With hours of practice, riding a bike is a skill that becomes automatic and can be done with minimal effort. For instance, when is the last time you thought about how much your body needed to lean in as you biked around a gradual curve? You typically don't think how much weight is needed to lean in to remain balanced around the turn, you simply do it. That's because riding a bike around a curve is a skill that you've practiced so much that it's automatic and you go on auto-pilot. The same concept applies to mental training. In the upcoming chapters, we'll discuss how to practice specific mental skills in detail.

Choosing a Practitioner

As a final comment, if and when you choose to work directly with a professional to improve your mental game, note that not all sport psychologists are trained the same way. There are two types of sport psychology coaches: clinical and educational. *Clinical sport psychologists* are licensed psychologists who treat individuals with emotional disorders as well as develop psychological skills to optimize performance. *Education sport psychologists,* on the other hand, are not licensed psychologists. Rather, they are professionals who foster positive psychological development in a population within a normal range of functioning. Educational sport psychologists develop mental skills with the intent of enhancing athletic performance as well as performance in other avenues of life. Neither type of sport psychologist is better. Rather, the service depends on an athlete's needs. Following are a few MST skills provided by a clinical sport psychologist verses those provided by an educational sport psychology coach:

Clinical Sport Psychologist

- Moderate to severe depression, anxiety, or anger
- Addictions
- Physical, mental, or emotional abuse
- Confidence, motivation, and sports performance

Educational Sport Psychology Coach/Mental Strength Coach

- Confidence and Motivation
- Goal setting
- Imagery
- Peak performance in sports and life

Summary

- Sport psychology is the scientific study of how the brain processes things (e.g., anxiety, confidence) and what one does about it (e.g., step forward or step back) within the context of sport.

- MST refers to the systematic approach of consistently practicing psychological skills to enhance performance and enjoyment in sports and life.
- The core psychological skills include motivation, goal setting, imagery, arousal control, stress management, and self-confidence. These skills promote optimal performance in sports, but are also skills that are transferable to all areas of life (e.g., public speaking, test taking, etc.)
- Myths of mental skills training include: (1) not enough time, (2) it's only for athletes who suffer severe-psychological disorders, and (3) it is a quick fix that will immediately improve sport performance.

References

Greenleaf, C., Gould, D., & Dieffenbach, K. (2001). Factors influencing Olympic performance: Interviews with Atlanta and Negano US Olympians. *Journal of Applied Sport Psychology, 13,* 154–184.

Heilman, C. (2017). How much of your sport is mental versus physical? Seven years' worth of opinions from youth to elite athletes and coaches during Mindset mental training sessions.

Johnson, B. (2017). *Destiny math: what you must be.* Written in Optimize newsletter April 6, 2017.

Krane, V., & Williams J. M. (2006). Psychological characteristics of peak performance. In J.M. Williams (ed.), *Applied sport psychology: Personal growth to peak performance* (5th ed., pp. 207–227). New York: McGraw-Hill.

Maslow, A. H., Frager, R., & Cox. R. (1970). In J. Fadiman, & C. McReynolds (eds.), *Motivation and personality* (Vol. 2, pp. 1997–1904). New York: Harper & Row.

Solomon, G. (2016). *Depression and suicide in athletes with sport-related concussions.* Presented at Big Sky Athletic Training and Sports Medicine Conference, February 3rd 2016.

Weinberg, R. S., & Gould, D. (2014). Introduction to psychological skills training. In *Foundations of Sport and Exercise Psychology, 6E* (pp. 249–271). Champaign, IL: Human Kinetics.

CHAPTER 2

Motivation: How to Light the Fire and Keep It Burning

"The difference between 'involvement' and 'commitment' is like an eggs-and-ham breakfast: the chicken was 'involved'—the pig was 'committed.'"

—Unknown

Based on this quote, which term is most closely associated with motivation, *involvement,* or *commitment*? Commitment! If you are committed, then you can do almost anything. Without commitment and motivation it is hard to find the inspiration to attain goals. That's why understanding motivation is the first essential step in building your mental skills toolkit. Motivation is the fuel that propels us along the path of excellence...day by day, week by week, and year by year. It is the foundation for pursuing excellence; thus, the reason why it is the first mental skill covered in this book.

What Is Motivation?

In the pursuit of excellence, the term *motivation* can be defined in a variety of ways. For instance, how would you describe your favorite athlete? Driven, disciplined, passionate, and tenacious? There are many words to describe motivation because it is expressed through our behaviors and actions. To encapsulate motivation, sport psychology researchers have described and distilled the essence of motivation into four common denominators: persistence, attitude, choice, and effort. The acronym PACE is an easy tool I created to help remember the definition of motivation (see Table 2.1).

Table 2.1 Defining motivation: PACE

P	Persistence	Consistently striving to attain a goal. Even in the face of adversity or when the deck is stacked against you, do you continually pursue your goals?
A	Attitude	Maintaining an open, positive perspective. How do you view challenges? Do challenges represent opportunities or are they barriers to success?
C	Choice	Making decisions. How do you prioritize your time? Do you seek out avenues to make yourself better, such as through adequate nutrition, recovery, gaining new knowledge, or improving relationships?
E	Effort	Trying hard. What's the amount of mental as well as physical intensity and enjoyment you put forth in training, competing, and achieving life goals? Even if you only feel like 60 percent, do you give every bit of 60 percent or are you tardy, distracted, or pessimistic when you don't feel your best?

Although the definition of motivation has been reduced down to four elements (PACE), it is a universal and complex issue within sports as well as life. There are many underlying reasons why motivation is expressed in a variety of ways but the positive influence of high levels of motivation is undeniable. Following is a scenario intended to describe the complexity of motivation and its relationship to success.

Alissa and Jenn are playing in a basketball tournament. As each of them dribble down the court in separate games, both Alissa and Jenn hear their family and friends cheering them on. Listening to the encouragement, Alissa enjoys striving harder in the game to make her friends, family, and herself proud. Alissa drives to the hoop and makes a layup. Jenn, on the other hand, gets nervous, losses focus, and passes the ball to the other team when she hears the cheers. This social encouragement motivates Alissa to excel while Jenn feels social pressure from the same cheering and falters.

Because motivation is influenced by so many personal and situational factors, there is no simple cookie-cutter approach to optimizing motivation. In this chapter, motivational theories and research will be introduced and applied. By the end of the chapter you will have a better idea of what motivates you as well as how to distill and identify what motivates others.

Motivation is a complex subject and can affect an athlete's performance and health in a multitude of ways

How to Light the Fire

Great athletes like Michael Phelps, Lindsey Vonn, and Phil Mickelson are all very talented. In addition to talent, they are also highly motivated and hard working. Without motivational drive most talented athletes don't reach their full potential. Even athletes who are NOT *gifted* can excel if they have the hunger, desire, and inspiration to do so. As NBA Hall of Famer Magic Johnson puts it, "Talent is never enough. With a few exceptions the best players are the hardest workers."

Understanding the factors that underlie motivation is an important aspect in fueling excellence. Motivational researcher, professor, and my mentor, Maria Newton, teaches sport psychology and describes the following important motivation regulators (personal communications, December 2016).

Two factors influencing motivation are:

1. How to light the fire
2. How to keep the fire burning.

A first step to improving motivation is understanding how to *Light the Fire*, meaning, what factors allow us to be the best version of ourselves. To better understand your motivators, take a minute to get out a pencil and piece of paper and write down the answers to the following Light the Fire exercise. Really! If you are serious about achieving peak levels of performance or you want to better understand how to help others reach their full potential, it's essential to understand personal motivation regulators. So take a moment and complete the following exercise.

Mental Exercise: Light the Fire

- How old were you when you began your sport or favorite activity?
- Why did you play your sport or activity?
- Why did you get so excited when you could go outside and play, go to practice, or have a game or rehearsal?

The aforelisted activities in the Light the Fire exercise, are typically the things you do for you. They usually are not competition-related. Rather, they are rewarding in and of themselves. Pleasure is usually the primary driver of why you do these things. When we think back to the beginning of our participation in sport or a specific activity, most individuals initially participate because it's fun. As skill development improves, there is a sense of pride that is felt as a result of working toward a goal. The sheer pleasure and inner satisfaction of learning and mastering a difficult skill represents a source of internal motivation. Internal motivators are especially important for sport enjoyment and performance and will be discussed in greater detail later in the chapter.

Many great performers, whether it's an elite athlete or successful entrepreneur, are a lot like the internally motivated beginner sport participant. They are *superb self-directed learners*. They practice diligently and seek out tools that make them a little better each day. Of course, there are examples of elite athletes and successful entrepreneurs who have prospered because they have taken advantage of others or committed crimes. Thus, being at the top of your game doesn't automatically make you a good person or make the world a better place. True champions, however, empower themselves and others to perform their best in sport—and life, so that they can positively impact themselves and the world. Vince Lombardi, the legendary coach of the Green Bay Packers, describes the fundamentals of motivation, the will to excel, and being a champion: "...I firmly believe that any man's finest hours—his greatest fulfillment of all that he holds dear—is that moment when he has worked his heart out in good cause and lies exhausted on the field of battle—victorious."

Thus, a key element to discovering and sustaining motivation is to be an internally driven, self-directed learner who finds pleasure, meaning, and purpose in a chosen endeavor (sport, exercise, or work). A good way to tap into the importance of a given endeavor is going back to when you first started participating and try to remember the pleasure, fulfillment, and commitment it gave you. This can help to *Light the Fire* because it connects us to the internal reasons of why we love to do whatever it is we do. But once the fire is lit it must be stoked.

How to Keep the Fire Burning

It's natural to go through peaks and valleys of motivation. Even the most talented athletes sometimes have trouble keeping the fire burning. Everyone has days when they feel like they have endless drive while other times they struggle to get out of bed in the morning.

To keep the motivational fire lit, it's helpful to do two things: first, go back to the reasons you just listed about why you got so excited when you first started your sport or activity (i.e., Light the Fire responses) and rewrite these reasons on a note card. When you experience a valley, feel stuck, or can't get out of a slump, which you inevitably will, remember why you first lit the fire. This simple reminder can renew your energy to not give up on what's important.

Second, connect to what deeply drives you *today*. Although there is some overlap between what motivates you today and what motivated you initially, greatness comes to people who *reflect on why* they remain passionate and the reasons that allow them to develop into the best version of themselves. As Brazilian soccer legend Pelé said, "Success is no accident. It takes hard work, perseverance, learning, studying, sacrifice and most of all, love of what you are doing or learning to do." Discover how to tap into the drive you have today by taking a moment to answer the following *Keep the Fire Burning* questions.

Mental Exercise: Keep the Fire Burning

- If you think about your sport or activity TODAY, why do you love it?
- What are the things that put a smile on your face…a twinkle in your eye…the fire in your heart that gets you excited to keep excelling?
- What does your sport or activity do for you? And WHY is that so important to you?

As you review your answers, you'll notice there are a variety of reasons why you remain motivated. Common reasons include:

- Recognition or winning
- Life meaning or bigger purpose
- Goal achievement
- Making money
- Mastering a skill
- Learning new things
- Encouragement to live your best life

Although everyone is motivated to participate in an activity for different reasons, what's common to us all is that we are driven to meet our individual needs (Deci & Ryan, 2010; Ryan & Deci, 2000). Understanding WHY we are motivated and what we need from our sport or activity is the *secret sauce* in helping us to reach our goals. For example, I participate in sports because it's a time when I feel free. I love pushing, playing, struggling, giggling, learning, improving, and experiencing life to its fullest. It's in these sport moments when I feel like I'm expressing the best version of myself. By experimenting with ways to be brave, face challenges, trust the process, and have fun within my sport, I discover strengths I never knew I had and I can learn to use these strengths within other life-contexts to become an overall better person. Thus, I keep the fire burning because my motivational mission is to *build a better me— and world, through sport.*

To really understand motivation we need to continually consider the reasons why we invest so much time and energy into our activities and how they feed our needs. The *Light the Fire* and *Keep the Fire Burning* exercises were meant to unravel why we are motivated. In the next section, the aim is to understand our psychological needs and how these basic needs can be met through the activities we choose.

At the Grand Teton Trail Marathon, myself (Christina Heilman) and other participants ran 26.2 miles on rugged trails at 6,000 to 10,000 feet elevation for the inner satisfaction in pursuing a goal that felt intrinsically worthwhile

Self-Determination Theory

Self-determination theory can be used as a tool to understand as well as optimize human behavior, motivation, and performance. According to the work of researchers Deci and Ryan (2000, 2010), self-determination is a multidimensional motivational theory modeled on the belief that we all have innate, basic psychological needs and we all have the intrinsic desire to engage in healthful and productive behaviors that will help us to meet these needs.

The three basic psychological needs are: autonomy, relatedness, and competence (ARC).

- The need for *autonomy* includes striving to feel like we have a choice or ownership over our behavior.
- The need for *relatedness* is striving to positively relate to others, belong to a group, or be cared for by others.
- The need for *competence* is striving to feel a sense of mastery, effectiveness, or understanding of a new skill.

The extent to which these needs (i.e., ARC) are or are not satisfied within an individual plays a vital role in performance and health. Within the context of sport participation, these needs can be satisfied by: (1) having choices as it pertains to training, practice, or competition (autonomy), (2) soliciting advice from athletes, coaches, or teammates or having others solicit advice from you (relatedness), and (3) feeling as if you have an important role on the team or as a member of the sporting community (competence). Creating a sport, or work, environment that serves to satisfy these needs will help an individual to function in a healthier and more productive way. To the extent that these needs are dissatisfied, such as an authoritative, controlling environment or being called an offensive name (e.g., *stupid, lazy, loser,* or even something as benign as *butter-fingers* in response to a player dropping a ball), individuals will show evidence of ill-being and non-optimal functioning (Ryan & Deci, 2000). For example, if an individual isn't allowed to be an active participant in choosing what they do each day, they lack autonomy which can lead to feelings of resentment or marginalization—and these feelings can be demotivating.

Self-determination theory can be used as a model for creating an environment that supports autonomy, relatedness, and competence as a way to promote curiosity, spiritedness, and self-motivation. When self-determined, athletes experience a sense of freedom to do what is personally interesting, important, and vitalizing. They are self-motivated and self-directed learners. If autonomy, relatedness, and competence are what we need to become more self-determined and internally motivated, then how do we foster this sort of environment? To better understand these concepts, brainstorm your ideas in the following mental exercise.

Mental Exercise: Self-Determination

The goal of this exercise is to brainstorm ways to create an environment that improves autonomy, relatedness, and competence so individuals can function in a healthy, productive way. To start, write down verbal and nonverbal cues as well as how you can use these cues to positively relate to, evaluate, communicate, teach, and embrace those around you (athletes, teammates, coaches, children, or anyone else that is important to you). For example, we can satisfy an individual's need for autonomy by providing a choice of what task they'd like to do in practice (i.e., set up practice equipment or put equipment away). Write down cues or actions in the following boxes that support an environment in which you and others feel autonomy, relatedness and competence.

Basic psychological needs	Actions that satisfy self-determination
Autonomy: Ability to act independently and accomplish a certain task to actively transform values into your own	
Relatedness: Ability to feel connected by something that has appeal of novelty, challenge, belonging or esthetic value	
Competence: Ability to learn or do something new and having a belief in your ability	

The purpose of the self-determination exercise was to gain a better understanding of how individuals use cues from their environment to influence whether their behavior is self-determined, which in turn influences motivation. As you review your answers, notice there are many ways self-determination can be enhanced through supportive experiences. For example, the need for relatedness might be met by creating and implementing team cohesion exercises. Competence could be satisfied by giving athletes adequate time to prepare for a competition or providing specific, constructive feedback while learning a new skill.

The preceding self-determination exercise may have also enlightened you to the difficulty of creating a purposefully self-determined environment. It is often difficult to think about interacting with others with the intent of trying to satisfy their basic psychological needs because it's a novel concept for most. Replacing old patterns with new skills takes time and effort. One way to help coaches create a self-determined environment for all team members is to collaborate with the athletes and other coaches and complete the aforementioned self-determination exercise. Conducting the self-determination exercise in a team setting can open doors of communication and optimize motivation for making positive and constructive changes. As the group shares responses, it can also empower athletes with a voice and choice that gives them a chance to articulate what they innately need from the sporting environment (autonomy and competence) and it provides an opportunity to connect with other teammates and coaches in a different way (relatedness).

In addition, improvement in sport performance requires the feedback, advice, and criticism from coaches and other athletes. Unfortunately, there are times when athletes are threatened by constructive criticism. The inability to give or accept constructive criticism doesn't support autonomy, relatedness, and competence. One practical and effective way to provide constructive criticism and foster self-determination is the *sandwich approach* (Smith & Smoll, 1996). The sandwich approach begins and ends the interaction on a positive note. This approach opens individuals to receiving future-oriented feedback and helps them remember the constructive criticism. The sandwich approach consists of three sequential steps:

1. A positive statement (i.e., Good effort!).
2. Future-oriented instructions (i.e., Next time you get nervous just take a deep breath and keep your eyes looking forward).
3. A compliment (i.e., Keep up the good work. You got this).

The sandwich approach begins and ends with supportive, positive statements but the critical element is the future-oriented instruction. The future-oriented instruction provides specific behaviors or techniques for the athlete to perform the next time that situation occurs. Future-oriented feedback helps the athlete focus on improving rather than dwelling on a past mistake, which can be discussed after the drill or game. The sandwich approach meets one's innate psychological needs and maximizes motivation because it encourages the athlete to accomplish a task (autonomy), connect to the coach (relatedness), and learn something new or gain a belief in his or her ability (competence).

Professional soccer player and coach, Drew DiCicco, delivers constructivce criticism to help players optimize self-determination and elevate their individualized potential

To summarize, self-determination theory seeks to understand what kinds of situations foster or hinder motivation by meeting, or not meeting, our basic psychological needs of autonomy, relatedness, and competence. These innate psychological needs are basic to everyone and are essential for ongoing growth, well-being, and achieving individualized potential. To the extent these needs are not satisfied, people will show evidence of ill-being (Deci & Ryan, 2000). In the next section, we explore how internal and external motivation is embedded into the self-determination theory as well as how the use of rewards can change our motivators.

Intrinsic and Extrinsic Motivation

Also rooted in self-determination theory is intrinsic and extrinsic motivation. From a general perspective, intrinsic motivation comes from the inside, whereas extrinsic motivation comes from the outside. Put another way, intrinsic motivation is internal and extrinsic motivation is external.

Intrinsic and extrinsic motivation can be viewed on a continuum (see Figure 2.1). On the left end of the continuum is amotivation (i.e., having no motivation or an *I don't care* attitude). At the opposite end of the spectrum is intrinsic motivation or an inherent passion and joy for a sport or an activity. In the middle of the continuum is external motivation, such as being motivated to earn money, get in better shape, win a championship, or accomplish a goal. Discussing the varying degrees of external motivation (i.e., external regulation, introjected behavior, and integrated regulation) is beyond the scope of this book, but Deci and Ryan's website www.selfdeterminationtheory.org is an excellent resource for further reading. Rather, in this text, we will deduce the multidimensional approach of motivation to the main contributing factors of intrinsic and extrinsic motivation.

If we are *intrinsically motivated* we do something because we gain satisfaction and joy as a result of engaging in a particular activity. For example, if someone plays a sport simply because he or she enjoys the activity then the individual will likely be intrinsically motivated to engage in the activity again. Intrinsic motivation is also about the excitement of gaining new knowledge or having the courage to test limits. Most of the reasons you listed in the *Light the Fire* exercise are likely derived from intrinsic motivation.

If we experience *extrinsic motivation*, then our drive to participate in a particular activity comes from an external source, such as trophies

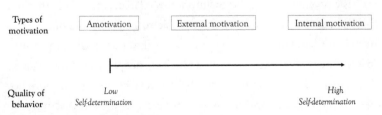

Figure 2.1 Self-determination continuum

or awards, money, social approval, losing weight, winning, or outdoing others. Essentially, if we are externally motivated we are trying to get something and the activity is a means to an end. Internal motivation, on the other hand, is an end in and of itself, it is the process we are seeking and we will do the activity for nothing in return.

To better understand intrinsic versus extrinsic motivation, review the previous *Light the Fire* and *Keep the Fire Burning* mental exercises, then complete the following exercise.

Mental Exercise: Evaluating Motives

- Review the lists you created from the previous *Light the Fire* and *Keep the Fire Burning* exercises.
- Using Table 2.2 as a guide, next to each reason you listed, label it with an *I* for intrinsic motivation or an *E* for extrinsic motivation.

Table 2.2 Examples of intrinsic and extrinsic motivators

Intrinsic	Extrinsic
Play sport because it is enjoyable	Play sport for a specific end result
Inner satisfaction	Social approval
Gain knowledge	Trophy
Excitement	Fear of punishment
Mastering a skill	Winning
Process is rewarding	Money
Enjoyment	Making a "team"

While reviewing your list of intrinsic and extrinsic motives for participating in a given activity, it's important to note that most athletes are motivated by both intrinsic and extrinsic factors. However, most exceptional athletes are only able to keep the fire lit if they are primarily intrinsically motivated and often remind themselves of those intrinsic motivators. Steven Kotler, an American journalist, entrepreneur, and author of one of my favorite sport performance books, *The Rise of Superman: Decoding the Science of Ultimate Human Performance*, puts it this way:

When doing what we most love transforms us into the best possible version of ourselves and that version hints at even greater future possibilities, the urge to explore those possibilities becomes feverish compulsion. Intrinsic motivation goes through the roof. Thus flow [in the zone, fully immersed and enjoying the process] becomes an alternative path to mastery, sans the misery.

Just to be clear, extrinsic motivators are not bad. But it is important to balance our extrinsic motivators with intrinsic ones. For instance, top athletes like Michael Jordan, Shaun White, and Serena Williams speak to the important role that fun, joy, and passion play in freeing them to excel. Research confirms greater performance, enjoyment, and persistence among youth to elite-level athletes occurs when they are primarily intrinsically versus extrinsically motivated (Ryan & Deci, 2007; Treasure, Lemyre, & Kuckzka, 2007). Athletes who only play to win are more likely to become quickly discouraged and not persevere long enough to reach their full potential.

Control and Competence: Want or Ought

Associating an activity with why we love it (intrinsic motivation) allows us to cultivate two key elements of motivation: *control and competence.* Control is when we feel like we are in the driver's seat and competence means we have a belief in our ability. When we feel in control and competent, we begin to see the many choices we have to optimize our performance and we are more self-determined. Ultimately, the difference between intrinsic and extrinsic motivation is determining if we are driven because we *want to* or because we *ought to.*

If we *want* to do something, then it's our choice. We are in control. When given a choice we see things in a positive light and we can bear almost anything. We *want* to play because it is fulfilling and we enjoy the process. This *want* increases intrinsic motivation and, thus, our ability to perform at a high level.

If we are driven by *ought*, then we often feel like we have no choice. We play because we *ought* to win the game, get the prize, or make the team. We feel trapped and forced to do the work and this decreases intrinsic motivation because the task is perceived as controlling. Intrinsic motivators provide a more stable and reliable source of fulfillment when compared to easy-come and easy-go external motivators, and as such, one might begin to wonder, "Does the use of extrinsic motivators, such as prizes or money, impact inherent intrinsic pleasure?"

After a training workout, an endurance athlete enjoys the inner pride that comes when choosing to work hard toward a goal; thus, fueling the control and competence required to optimize performance and personal excellence

Do Rewards Undermine Motivation?

We live in a world of extrinsic motivators: scholarships, public recognition, bonuses, and all-star trophies. Thus, it is important to understand how external rewards can help or hinder our efforts to improve motivation.

Research has found that extrinsic rewards often backfire (Deci, 1971; Kohn, 1999; Pink, 2011). We may think that rewards, trophies, or money instill greater intrinsic motivation, but rewards actually undermine motivation if not administered appropriately. Lepper and Greene's classic study *Turning Play Into Work* illustrates how rewards undermine intrinsic motivation.

In a Lepper and Greene (1975) study, preschool children drew pictures with felt pens, an activity considered intrinsically enjoyable. Each child was asked to draw under one of three reward conditions (see Table 2.3). In the *expected reward* condition, children expected to win a highly attractive toy by agreeing to draw a picture. In the *unexpected reward* condition, children had no prior knowledge of this reward. Instead the toy was given to the children after they had drawn the picture. In the *no reward* condition, the children neither anticipated nor received an award for drawing the picture.

Two weeks later, the children were monitored through cameras and observed for their interest in the same drawing activity in a free-choice situation. The findings showed that the children who had drawn expecting an extrinsic reward showed less interest in the subsequent drawing activity and, thus, a decrease in intrinsic motivation compared to those who had not expected a reward. The unexpected reward and no-reward group had drawn just as much as they had the first time. This study was one of the first to example the importance of understanding the potential long-term effects of extrinsic reward as well as *how* rewards are administered and the subsequent intrinsic motivation toward an activity.

Table 2.3 Three conditions in the Lepper and Greene (1975) study turning work into play

Conditions	Reward	Free choice: Observed interest in drawing
Expected reward	Expected to win a toy for drawing a picture	Drew less and showed less interest in drawing compared to children who had not expected a reward
Unexpected reward	Unexpectedly given a toy after drawing a picture	Drew just as much as they had the first time
No reward	No toy given after drawing a picture	Drew just as much as they had the first time

Further research based on the *Turning Work Into Play* findings show external rewards undermine intrinsic motivation but only under certain circumstances (Eisenberger & Cameron, 1996, Vallerand, Deci, & Ryan,

1987). The impact of external rewards on intrinsic motivation is dependent on how the individual *perceives* the reward.

Perceptions of awards are determined if they are viewed as:

- More or less controlling
- More or less competent

To better understand the use of *control* NBA player Magic Johnson shares his story of being recruited to play college basketball. Magic Johnson: "I received my share of offers for cars and money. It immediately turned me off. It was like they [college coaches] were trying to buy me, and I didn't like anyone trying to buy me" (Weinberg, 1984). Johnson perceived the offerings of money and cars as someone trying to buy him. That *perception* undermined his intrinsic love for playing basketball because it felt like someone was trying to control him with the promise of material gifts. Hence, extrinsic rewards viewed as manipulative, bribing, or controlling have the potential to undermine intrinsic motivation.

Rewards can also lower intrinsic motivation if they squash an athlete's sense of *competence*. This often occurs when the reward communicates something negative about the athlete's ability or contribution to the team, such as calling an athlete clumsy when he or she was giving 100 percent effort or striving for the MVP (i.e., most valuable player) reward and not receiving it.

Can Rewards Foster Motivation?

Extrinsic rewards can instill intrinsic motivation and help athletes feel successful if they *raise perceived control and competence*. These rewards include: a verbal recognition of one's effort, a sign of encouragement on a locker while striving to reach a meaningful goal, or a pat on the back for helping out a teammate with an unexpected challenge.

Rewards not based on actions or that do not convey anything positive to the athlete's ability have no power in enhancing intrinsic motivation. Rather, rewards need to be personalized so that each athlete understands the specific contribution he or she makes to the team or his or her chosen endeavor. Rewards should provide athletes with meaningful information and feedback which allows them to feel more in control and competent in the things they are striving for, thus, fueling intrinsic motivation and self-determination.

The key is to provide rewards that sincerely recognize the things athletes do well and the effort put forth. As an example, I worked with a collegiate cross country and track coach, Deb Vercauteren, who guided her athletes to 17 NCAA Division III team titles. Vercauteren's success was due in part to her recognition of each runner's level of effort, sportspersonship, attitude, and unique contributions by providing specific feedback within each athlete's training journal. Each day the runners were expected to draw, paint, write, or create a reflective piece in their training journal. One day a week, Vercauteren would collect everyone's journals, read them, and provide individualized comments on how to improve training, develop a winning mindset, or become the happiest, strongest version of themselves. Vercauteren's personalized feedback was not based in being a physically skilled athlete, rather it was rooted in character, such as being optimistic, determined, or willingness to help out. This kind of sincere recognition is an example of giving an athlete a personalized reward that encourages motivation and boosts performance.

If done right, extrinsic rewards can instill intrinsic motivation. Another coaching-related example includes a coach who provides the team with a reward for completing a *no-fun* drill and slowly deemphasize the reward as athletes begin to see the inherent benefits of the exercise. Another example may include the novice runner who is motivated to lose weight (an extrinsic motivator). This individual might give him or herself a reward, such as putting money in a jar for each training day or each pound lost. Over time, they may find themselves enjoying running—even craving it. They started running for an extrinsic reason (to lose weight) and rewarded themselves with money. As they progressed with their training, running turned out to be internally rewarding as well.

Rewards don't have to be big. They even can be simple and silly. For instance, you can award a *bottle of glue* to the player who kept it together despite adversity they faced that week. A coach could give an athlete the *nail award* for the person who nails a drill with good execution and effort. In my ski patrol unit, we have a *bulldog award* for the person who provided first aid services to most number of injured guests. The recipient of the bulldog award doesn't receive an actual bulldog, rather, the winner receives recognition at the end of the season ski patrol party with a bulldog sticker to put on his or her ski helmet.

Rewards are tricky. Because we now better understand that perceived competence and control is what fosters or undermines intrinsic motivation, I challenge you to think about any reward you received or will give to yourself or someone else in the future. In the following mental exercise, ask yourself the following questions before giving a reward.

Mental Exercise: Impact of Rewards

- What does this reward mean? Did I receive the reward because it came from something I did?
- Does this reward control me and undermine the internal reasons of why I love what I do?
- Does this reward give me information on my competence or my ability to grow and improve?

If an extrinsic reward comes from something we did, if it doesn't control us, and if it provides information on our ability, then this helps us to develop intrinsic motivation, growth, and self-determination. Rewards are meant to recognize an athlete's actions despite if they win or lose because on the journey of elevating your excellence sometimes you win and sometimes you learn.

It's also important to remember that although recognition, trophies, and medals are nice tokens of our efforts and abilities, the ultimate reward is a sense of success in striving for something we felt was worthwhile (remember the *Light the Fire* exercise). Champion athletes and coaches deeply understand and value the concept of the inner pride and enthusiasm that comes when working hard toward mastering a skill, accomplishing a goal, or having satisfaction derived from an experience. As NBA Hall of Famer, Larry Bird said, "I've got a theory that if you give 100 percent all of the time, somehow things will work out in the end."

Success, then, is not the reward. Self-referencing or basing achievements on personal standards, such as improvement, satisfactory effort, task mastery, personal development, and enjoying the experience, is the ultimate reward. In the following chapter we'll learn another key component of the mindset and methods that make champions: How to set and achieve goals.

Summary

- Motivation is defined by PACE: Persistence. Attitude. Commitment. Effort.
- A key element to motivation is finding pleasure and meaning in sport, exercise, or work. It's connecting to the deep, intrinsic reasons of why we love what we do that will lead us along the path of excellence…day by day, week by week, and year by year.
- Self-determination theory is a multidimensional view in how to optimize human behavior. The three primary psychological needs that are basic to every human being are autonomy, relatedness, and competence. You must feed your needs to achieve your individual potential.
- The sandwich approach is a coaching method to provide constructive feedback in a supportive, effective manner that improves athlete motivation and self-determination. The sandwich approach involves three sequential steps: (1) a positive statement, (2) future-oriented instructions, and (3) a compliment.
- Intrinsically motivated athletes are self-determined and play for the love of the game. They enjoy the inner pride and accomplishment that comes when working hard toward a goal, mastering a skill, or fully enjoying the process.
- Extrinsically motivated athletes participate primarily for social approval, awards, money, winning, or outdoing others.
- Intrinsic motivation results in better performance, enjoyment, and persistence compared to extrinsic motivation.
- Rewards can increase or decrease intrinsic motivation.
- Extrinsic rewards increase intrinsic motivation if they raise perceived control and competence (i.e., meaningful and specific rewards about effort or contribution to the team, personalized feedback).

- If extrinsic rewards lower perceived control and competence (i.e., generalized comments, striving for an award and not receiving it, feeling "bought-out"), then extrinsic rewards will undermine intrinsic motivation.

References

Deci, E. L. (1971). Effects of externally mediated rewards on intrinsic motivation. *Journal of Personality and Social Psychology, 18,* 105–115.

Deci, E. L., & Ryan, R. M. (2010). *Self-determination.* John Wiley & Sons, Inc..

Eisenberger, R., & Cameron, J. (1996). Detrimental effects of reward: Myth or reality? *American Psychologist, 51,* 1153–1166.

Kohn, A. (1999). *Punished be rewards: The trouble with gold stars, incentive plans, A's, praise, and other bribes.* Boston: Houghton Mifflin.

Kotler, S. (2014). *The rise of superman: Decoding the science of ultimate human performance.* Houghton Mifflin Harcourt.

Lepper, M. R., & Greene, D. (1975). Turning play into work: Effects of adult surveillance and extrinsic rewards on children's intrinsic motivation. *Journal of Personality and Social Psychology, 31,* 479–486.

Pink, D. H. (2011). *Drive: The surprising truth about what motivates us.* Penguin.

Ryan, R. M., & Deci, E. L. (2007). Active human nature self-determination theory and the promotion and maintenance of sport, exercise and health. In M. S. Hagger and N. Chatzisarantis (eds.), *Intrinsic motivation and self-determination in exercise and sport* (pp. 1–19). Champaign, IL: Human Kinetics.

Ryan, R. M., & Deci, E. L. (2000). Self-determination theory and the facilitation of intrinsic motivation, social development and well-being. *American Psychologist, 55,* 68–78.

Smith, R. E., & Smoll, F. L. (1996). *Way to go, coach: A scientifically-proven approach to coaching effectiveness.* Portola Valley, CA: Warde.

Treasure, D. C., Lemyre, P. N., & Kuckzka, K. (2007). Motivation in elite-level sport a self-determination perspective. In M. S. Hagger and N. Chatzisarantis (eds.), *Intrinsic motivation and self-determination in exercise and sport* (pp. 153–165). Champaign, IL: Human Kinetics.

Vallerand, R. J., Deci, E., & Ryan, R. M. (1987). Intrinsic motivation in sport. Exercise and Sport Sciences Reviews, 389–425.

Weinberg, R. S. (1984). The relationship between extrinsic rewards and intrinsic motivation in sports. In J. M. Silva & R. S. Weinberg (eds.), *Psychological foundations of sport* (pp. 177–187). Champaign, IL: Human Kinetics.

CHAPTER 3

Goal Setting: Achieving Big Dreams and Bold Goals

"The most successful athletes all have one thing in common. They set specific goals and strive to achieve them."
—Damon Burton, Sports Psychology Scholar

Goal setting is among the most effective mental skill used to enhance sport performance. In reviewing published research related to goal setting in sport and physical activity, Burton (2008) reported that more than three-quarters of studies found that goal setting produced positive results. Goal setting is arguably the most effective tool that we can use to change behaviors and it is the changes in our daily behaviors and actions which lead to big improvements in sport performances. Importantly, the goal setting process is beneficial not only for enhancing athletic performance, but also for improving interpersonal relationships, academics, job performance, and physical and mental well-being.

Many of us understand the idea of goal setting, but few of us reach the goals we set out to achieve. This is likely due to several factors related to a poor understanding of the goal-setting process. The better we understand the fundamentals of goal setting the more we can benefit from using goals. This chapter focuses on basic goal-setting fundamentals as well as applications and strategies to reach those goals.

Sport performance-related goals can be partitioned into those related to training and those related to competition. The primary focus of this chapter pertains to setting and achieving training goals. Training goals are highlighted because athletes spend a considerable amount of time training to improve techniques and skills as well as develop strength, power, and endurance. As such, before athletes set competition goals, they must first achieve their predetermined training goals.

Understanding Goals

According to Ed Locke, a pioneering researcher on goal setting, goals can be defined as, *"attaining a specific standard of proficiency on a task, usually with a specified time limit...it is an object or aim of an action"* (Locke et al., 1981, p. 126).

More enthusiastically defined: *Goals are our dreams.* Having a goal is to set an intention or have a vision of who we want to become, what we want to accomplish, or how we want to perform. Moreover, goals give us direction toward our dreams, attract us to new possibilities, remain optimistic despite adversity, and strengthen our purpose (Vernacchia, 2003).

Goals also provide a standard for measuring progress and remind us of the specific strides, both short and long terms, we need to take in the journey toward success. By measuring this progress we can see, little by little, how we are getting closer to our goals. This increases our ability to focus on the task, improves effort toward mastery, and helps us to find the joy in the journey (Burton & Weiss, 2008; Locke, 1996).

When we set goals, we also recognize a valuable tool...when we're off track. This awareness helps us to analyze and correct barriers, maintain commitment, and remain hopeful despite adversity.

If we don't set goals, then we often forget to recognize the little accomplishments along the pathway to success. As a result, we experience less joy, we lose focus, our optimism declines and we can no longer see dreams as a reality (Weinberg & Gould, 2014). When we forget to pause and celebrate small wins the goal simply becomes too overwhelming to achieve and we stop trying because we can't see progress. Thus, success in achieving goals is a byproduct of small wins. Every choice we make throughout the day is key in reaching a goal.

Goals: Climbing a Mountain

The process of climbing a mountain is a good metaphor for setting and achieving goals. First, we start with the end in mind—reaching a dreamy mountain top. If the end goal is to get to the top of the mountain, then we need to develop a plan of short-term goals and a route to get there. The route up the mountain will likely have unexpected twists and turns.

In order to continue on the journey, these unanticipated obstacles will require that we remain flexible in our approach and fine-tune our strategies along the way, we may even need to find a different path to the top. By modifying goals and evaluating and adjusting our actions when necessary, we can maintain motivation and momentum (no matter how small those steps around obstacles may be) and reach the dreamy mountain top.

To quote Edmund Hillary the first climber to summit Mount Everest, "It is not the mountain we conquer but ourselves." The first step in conquering our goals and climbing to our dreams is *understanding the characteristics of effective goals.*

Maintaining motivation, being flexible, and modifying the plan if necessary are required to accomplish a goal (summit of the Middle Teton)

Choosing Effective Goals

Effective goals motivate athletes and passionate professionals to maximize their potential. Goal setting energizes individuals to become more productive. Goals increase efficiency, boost self-confidence, and empower us to persist in the face of adversity and failure (Locke, 1996; Tamminen et al., 2014). The specific benefits of setting a goal are dependent on the type of goal(s) set. *There are three general types of goals:*

1. Outcome
2. Performance
3. Process

Outcome Goals

Outcome goals are long-term goals. They focus on the end result, like winning, making the varsity team, or outperforming a competitor. Outcome goals may be beneficial because they can motivate us to give more effort in the short term. However, outcome goals are generally not effective if they are not paired with more extensive short-term goals. This is because attainment of the outcome goal isn't achievable until the distant future and sometimes depends on how others perform (Kyllo & Landers, 1995). The key to attaining the long-term outcome goal is continually emphasizing performance and process goals.

When achievement of an outcome goal, such as winning a soccer tournament or placing in a climbing competition, depends on how others perform then the goal is out of the athlete's control. As discussed in the previous chapter on motivation, things that are outside of our control decreases motivation because no matter the effort we put in, the end result is dependent on how others perform or weather conditions. Additionally, if an athlete only focuses on the final outcome, the end result doesn't always allow them to take credit for success and improvement along the way. Athletes who set only outcome goals (i.e., winning, making a specific team, earning an award, getting to the top of the mountain), consciously or subconsciously, feel a lack of control over their own success and as a result, experience more performance anxiety, apathy, and loss of concentration (Adie, Duda & Ntoumanis, 2008; Burton, 1989). It has also long been known that athletes who base their self-worth on outcome goals tend to feel more helpless and their self-confidence is often unstable because there is only one winner or one end result and anything else might be considered a failure (Weiner, 1985).

Outcome goals are not inherently detrimental but placing a very high emphasis on them, especially during competition, can decrease instead of enhance performance (Weinberg & Gould, 2014). In achieving the long-term outcome goal, it is important to take progressive strides toward short-term goals that are within your control. The next section outlines how performance and process goals provide specific steps to reach your outcome goals and, consequently, optimize performance.

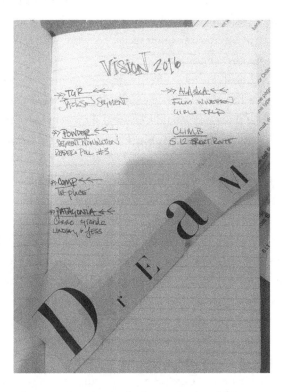

Outcome goals wrote in a journal of a professional big mountain skier and aspiring mountaineer

Performance and Process Goals

Focusing on performance and process goals is an effective means to help athletes remain motivated, confident, and moving toward their mountain top outcome goal. Performance and process goals differ from outcome goals because they are short-term goals and dependent upon self-referenced behaviors. It is performance and process goals that ultimately help us achieve the outcome goal.

Performance goals focus on improvements and can be compared to an athlete's previous performance. *Examples of performance goals include*: increasing the number of stolen bases, improving the number of shots taken to the hockey goal, achieving a personal best in the 5K race, or placing better in a cross country ski race. Performance goals are based on personal standards of success. Sometimes performance goals are partially dependent on others as a basis of comparison to one's past performance. For example, a performance goal of placing better in a cross country ski race is dependent on how the other racers perform, who is competing at the race, and weather conditions.

Performance goals are more effective than outcome goals because they tend to be more flexible and more within one's control. Hence, for each outcome goal set there also should be several short-term performance and process goals that lead to the outcome (Filby, Maynard & Graydon, 1999; Weinberg & Butt, 2014).

Process goals refer to the achievement or improvement of specific skills, behaviors, and actions. These goals are set in an effort to achieve consistent results and learn the skills necessary to optimize performance. Setting and achieving process goals allows the athlete to reach performance goals. *Examples of process goals include:* practicing a pre-shot free-throw routine for 5 minutes three times a week after practice, running speed drills twice a week, increasing resistance training frequency to four times a week, practicing maintaining a positive headspace after a mistake, planning out tactical strategies for common scenarios in competition, properly rehydrating and fueling after training, improving attitude during training sessions, and adhering to the weekly training program.

Process goals are effective because athletes can achieve them in a shorter period of time and achievement is not dependent on the actions of others. Athletes can see themselves chipping away at their long-term and outcome goals by making small daily tweaks that, over time, improve mental and physical performance. Achieving process goals also serves to increase confidence, satisfaction, and decreases worry about performing *perfectly* (Jones & Hanton, 1996; Nicholls, Perry, & Calmeiro, 2014).

Although extremely useful, performance and process goals can be problematic because they are often hard to prioritize and, if not properly articulated, almost impossible to quantify. For example, it takes determination and discipline to prioritize mundane running drills or to shoot free-throws after a challenging training session. Additionally, it is difficult to measure goals such as *improved running efficiency* or *keeping a positive headspace after a mistake.* If an athlete can put the goal into quantifiable terms and see the connection between the process goal and the performance goal as well as the overall outcome goal, it is likely they will be more motivated to engage in and maintain the goal behavior. Details on setting goals into quantifiable, measurable ways are discussed in the next section.

As a review, the following examples show how outcome, performance, and process goals are related.

Example 1: A high school golfer hopes to earn an athletic scholarship to a Division One University, this represents an outcome goal. The associated performance goal is to lower the score by five strokes per game. By achieving this goal the player is much more likely to be offered a scholarship. However, in order to improve game-day performance, this player must first make process goals that will facilitate improvements in golf swing accuracy. In order to improve golf swing accuracy this athlete will likely have to set several process goals that will improve physical and mental capacities, such as carving out time before practice to refine a pre-shot routine or taking time before bed to visualize a game where the athlete plays optimally and easily lowers golf strokes by five points or more. These process goals are daily behaviors and actions that will allow for performance improvement and the attainment of the athlete's outcome goal.

Example 2: To win a local 5K race (outcome goal), a female runner has to be able to finish faster than the last years fastest runner, <20 minutes or <6:26 per mile pace (performance goal). To achieve the performance goal, she sets a series of process goals that focus on improved technique, strength, and endurance, such as running 6:25 minute per mile repeats on Mondays and 400-meter intervals in <1:30 minutes on Wednesdays.

Achieving performance and process goals breeds a special kind of confidence, fulfillment, and sense of accomplishment that stays with the athlete, regardless of winning or losing. Take 28-year-old Brenda Martinez courageous story of making it to the 2016 Olympics as an example.

At the 2016 United States Track and Field Olympic Qualifier, Brenda Martinez was in position to win the 800-meter race. A trailing runner tripped causing Martinez to fall and lose her spot on the Olympic team. Martinez could have wallowed and felt sorry for herself. Yet, Martinez responded to reporters, "The track doesn't care about your feelings. You've just got to move forward." Less than a week later, Martinez ran in the 1,500-meter and won a spot to go to the Olympics in Rio. Rather than being attached to her goal of making the Olympic team in her best event, the 800-meter, Martinez focused on the process. She said, "I just quickly let go of what happened in the 800-meter and got back to my routine, to focusing on all the little things I could do that would give me the best chance of running well later in the week."

This scenario is an example of how outcome goals can be out of the athlete's control. In this situation Martinez could have easily crumbled under the distress caused by not making the Olympic Team, instead, she hit the reset button and focused on positive performance-enhancing behaviors that she could control. Outcome, performance, and process goals each contribute to success in sports.

Unfortunately, most athletes and coaches that I work with only set outcome goals. Why? Because they are straightforward. Whether you win or lose is easy to see. The irony is that the performance and process goals get you to the outcome but these are the toughest to write and measure. The next section outlines six goal characteristics that are associated with achieving performance and process goals.

Although each type of goal (outcome, performance, and process) contributes to success in sports, most athletes neglect to prioritize the small but essential, daily process goals, such as completing a bike training session by forging a creek

Setting S.M.A.R.T. Goals

Although there are several methodologies used to achieve goals, the mnemonic S.M.A.R.T. is an easy tool to help foster performance gains in sports and all areas of life. *S.M.A.R.T. stands for:*

- Specific
- Measureable
- Action-oriented
- Realistic
- Timely

Set Specific Goals

Goals can range from vague to specific. An example of a vague goal is *try your hardest*. Although this is a great goal because it's within your control, it is also inexact. Vague goals are often too general to establish a criterion to measure the quality and consistency of one's performance. The more specific a goal, the more likely an individual is to continually progress to achieve that goal because there will be small victories along the way to achieving larger, long-term performance and outcome goals.

Specific goals define purpose and actions to accomplish. Specific goals identify clear expectations and define precisely what needs to be done so athletes and coaches understand the steps needed to reach the goal. Examples include:

- Incorporate two weekly speed and agility sessions into the warm-up routine.
- Drink at least 8 ounces of water before and immediately after practice.
- Improve knee range of motion by five degrees by doing physical therapy every day.
- Increase the number of passes before a shot to the hockey goal by 10 percent.
- Improve daily effort in practice from a 6 on a 1 to 10 point scale to an 8.

Set Measurable Goals

Goals are best accomplished when an individual has a way to *measure the goal and make strides toward the goal.* Without this data, it's hard to identify what's working and what's not working. A goal that is measurable is quantifiable, such as percentages, time, inches, pounds, or even using a 1 to 10 scale to subjectively quantify behaviors and actions. Examples of measurable goals include:

- Decreasing giant slalom ski time by 5 seconds
- Improving the number of shots taken to the lacrosse goal by 5 percent
- Increasing current pass rate by 10 percent
- Improving mental acuity by visualizing for 5-minutes before practice
- Eating at least five servings of fruit and vegetable daily

A good way to measure more elusive behavioral goals, such as effort or sportspersonship, is with a subjective scale of 1 to 10 (1 = no effort, 10 = lots of effort) or a Likert scale (1 = strongly disagree, 5 = strongly agree). In the previous section on specific goals, I gave an example of a goal behavior or attitude (improve daily effort in practice) that could be measured with a numeric scale (increase from a 6 on a 1 to 10 point scale to an 8).

As an applied example of using a subjective scale, a middle school basketball coach I worked with set daily behavioral goals by recording each player's level of effort as well as having the players measure their perceived level of effort at the end of every practice. Those who put forth the most effort in practice for the week were the starters for the upcoming game. The coach valued effort, which was within the player's control, and he rewarded the players who put forth effort with playing time. This is a great example of how to set and measure a specific behavioral goal, as well as how to provide an appropriate reward as a motivator.

Great athletes know if they are achieving their goals because they frequently measure and keep track of positive and negative changes related to those goals. When athletes keep score they better understand the connection between their effort and subsequent performance as well as their overall ability to reach the outcome goal. Knowing the score raises the level of play because the athlete can determine what is working and what adjustments need to be made. This kind of information inspires and motivates the athlete to continue toward reaching the goal—even on the days they don't feel like it.

Middle distance runner, physician, and Englishmen, Roger Bannister, is a great example of applying measurable goals to achieve an outcome goal. During the 1950s, physiology researchers claimed that it was physically impossible to break the 4-minute mile. Bannister wasn't so sure. Bannister started breaking down his dream of running a mile in under 4-minutes by setting manageable training goals. He trained until he could run his first quarter mile in under a minute or less. Then, he trained until he could run a half mile in under 2 minutes. Next, he trained until he could run three-fourth of a mile in under 3 minutes. Finally, Roger ran quarter mile repeats under a minute. On May 6, 1954 in Oxford England, Roger ran a 3:59.4 mile. He achieved an impossible goal by breaking it down into palatable pieces that he could measure. Sixty years later, this is still one of the most iconic sport moments in history.

How about you? What's your big outcome goal and how can it be broken down into a bite-size, feasible, and measurable goals? As Henry Ford once said, "Nothing is particularly hard if you break it into enough small pieces."

In setting measurable goals, questions to can ask yourself are:

- How can I quantitatively measure my goal?
- How will I keep track of changes associated with my goal?
- How can I keep a daily scorecard of steps I'm taking toward reaching my goal (mark a graph, record on a calendar, use a spreadsheet)?

Set Action-Oriented Goals

People tend to focus too much on where they are going (outcome goal) and don't look closely enough at *how* they are going to get there. This is one of the main problems people run into when setting a goal because it's the *actions* that lead us to our outcome goals. It is important to identify the outcome goal because it serves as a motivator but outcome goals cannot stand alone.

Action-oriented goals tell us that something needs to be done. For example, if I'm trying to improve my level of effort in practice from a 6 to an 8 on a scale of 1 to 10, then a daily action step would include writing down my level of effort after each drill and average the score at the end of practice. If my goal is to eat seven fruits and vegetables each day, then the action step might include going to the grocery store over the weekend to buy fresh fruits and vegetables for the week, prepping meals on Sunday, or logging daily food intake into an app like myfitnesspal.

Another common missing piece in setting action-oriented goals is the language we use. It's essential to write and say the goal as if we've already accomplished it. Rather than saying, "I will eat seven fruits and vegetables today," it's important to rephrase this statement and say "Each day I *eat* seven servings of fruits and vegetables." The *will* in the first sentence tells your brain that this behavior is something you're going to do in the future and, thus, you put it off and it never happens (Helmstetter, 1990). Saying your goal in the *present tense* "I eat..." sets an intention and sends a message to your brain that this is something you do right now. Thus, you're programming your brain to take action.

Also, remember to set action-oriented goals in a positive way rather than negative. *Positive goals* tend to foster self-confidence and intrinsic motivation because you focus on what you hope to accomplish rather than what you want to avoid. In creating positive goals, refrain from using adverse language such as not or don't (e.g., don't mess up the big game). Rather use language that uplifts and inspires you as well as evokes a visceral response (e.g., empower, encourage, allow, rise up, believe, trust). For example, instead of writing "I don't want my body weight to be too heavy for competition" (or even "I want to lose weight" which can be perceived as deprivation), write, "I create daily healthy habits that keep me fit, fast, and strong. My daily habits are drinking 100 ounces of water per day, eating at least 7 servings of fruits and vegetables today, and enjoy journaling in my training log for 5-minutes after practice." Writing down what you want in specific, action-oriented, and positive-focused ways helps you to achieve your goals.

If you feel stuck and don't know what action to take, then ask yourself, "What is the smallest, simplest, and easiest step I can take to help me reach my goal right now?"

As skiers tour underneath the Moose's Tooth in the Alaska Range, it's key to use S.M.A.R.T. (specific, measurable, action-oriented, realistic, and timely) goals in training as way to help them achieve their big outcome goals. (PC: Mike Leake)

Set Realistic Goals

Research suggests goals that are moderate in difficulty promote the greatest gains in performance (Burton & Weiss, 2008; Kyllo & Landers, 1995). Goals that are too difficult create tension, stress, and loss of motivation because we stretch ourselves too far. Yet, if goals are too easy we tend to get bored and lose interest. Goals that are just slightly out of reach encourages commitment, sparks inspiration, and minimizes stress, which aids in persisting toward a goal—even when the road becomes bumpy.

How difficult should a goal should be? A realistic goal should be adjusted to reflect capabilities given various constraints (e.g., work deadlines, time to train, injuries). Taking time to write down our constraints, doubts, and potential obstacles helps us to better understand if our goal is realistic and prevents us from being overly optimistic, a common pitfall that results in unachievable goals. Highlighting what we might be avoiding helps to set realistic goals and avoid unintentionally sabotaging goals. Gabrielle Oettingen (2012, 2015), a leading researcher and author in studying the science of making your dreams a reality, suggests WOOP as a way to set realistic goals:

- W is for wish (outcome goal, what do you want to achieve).
- O is for outcome (benefits, what do you want to experience when that wish is present).
- O is for obstacles (constraints, what potential pitfalls will you face).
- P is for plan (action steps, how do you deal with obstacles and reach your wish).

At the heart of WOOP is creating a plan to overcome obstacles. Oettingen calls the plan to get over, under, or across obstacles as *implementation intentions*, which includes anticipating challenges and how to deal with them in advance. To deal with obstacles, Oettingen suggests if, then statements: If x happens, then I will do y. For example, if I miss a workout, then I'll let it go and be nice to myself. And, WOOP there it is… you're off achieving your goals.

Another popular tool I use to assess if athletes or exercisers are setting moderately difficult goals is a subjective confidence scale. On a scale of 1 to 10, one being not confident and 10 being fully confident, how confident are you in reaching your goal? If the answer is around seven, then it is a moderately challenging goal. If the answer is below seven, then the goal is likely too difficult. To avoid a set-up for failure, the goal should be adjusted to be more manageable. On the other hand, a score of 10 signifies the goal is probably too easy and will likely not spark the inspiration and commitment needed to accomplish the goal. Determining if goals are realistic on a subjective confidence scale of 1 to 10 is anecdotal, however, it is a helpful exercise that can be used to acknowledge one's ability, which is a robust predictor to performance and goal attainment (Jones & Hanton, 1996).

The takeaway from this section is to set moderately difficult goals that are challenging and exciting, yet realistic. It is a goal that is just outside of your comfort zone.

Set Timely Goals

A timely goal refers to achieving a goal within a reasonable time frame. If there is not a deadline, it is likely efforts will be postponed. Set a deadline but be flexible in the event of unanticipated hiccups, hurdles, and holes. If it is unclear how long it will take to achieve a goal, try reverse engineering. Reverse engineering refers to determining the end date and, then, working backwards to outline each step needed to reach the goal.

In a goal-setting workshop I conducted, a participant reverse engineered her book deadline and realized that it was going to take her nearly twice as long as expected. This realization was incredibly helpful to her because knowing that the goal was too ambitious relieved the stress of meeting her self-imposed deadline. She reset the book deadline to a more feasible date and at the end of the workshop expressed being more motivated and inspired to move forward writing her book.

Making Goals Work

Goal setting is an important skill that requires many elements to be used optimally. To help put all the pieces together, Figure 3.1 is an easy, effective tool to help summarize the goal setting process.

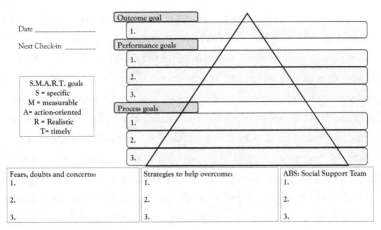

Figure 3.1 Goal setting pyramid

Seek Social Support

In addition to S.M.A.R.T. goals, a key element in attaining goals is creating a strong social support system. A social support system includes a team of people who positively contribute to an individual's goals and are available to listen to new ideas and brainstorms. These individuals should back your efforts and be your cheerleader regardless of success or struggle. A support system could include: loved ones, coworkers, teammates, friends, or a coach or athletic trainer. I like to call these individuals my Accountability Buddy System (ABS).

With a good support system, you don't have to do it all by yourself. For instance, when I told my ABS that I was writing this book, one of the first things they would ask me was, "How's the book?" This network of people held me accountable and offered suggestions during the process of writing, even when I took a 2-month break from this book…twice. How about you—who do you want on your team?

Think It and Ink It

Writing down goals and why each is valuable makes goals attainable. On the days filled with insecurity and self-doubt, reviewing goals helps an individual to avoid losing confidence in their abilities. To battle the ebb and flow, writing down *why* a goal is meaningful and going back to it when faith falters is a way to spark the necessary inspiration to reach a goal. Remember, *"No matter how slow you're going you're still lapping everyone on the couch"*—Unknown. Progress, no matter how small, is still progress.

The act of writing down a goal also activates a chemical reaction in the brain that is different from simply thinking about a goal. Putting goals on paper also allows a more concrete idea of what one wants to achieve and the steps necessary to live that vision. For example, a professional mountain athlete shared with me that one of the best mental tools I taught him was to write down his goals each morning on a mirror with a dry erase marker. After writing down the goal, I recommended he erase it so that he can rewrite it tomorrow and solidify his ideal vision as an athlete and as a person. As this athlete travels the world for climbing, skiing, and mountaineering, he takes his dry erase marker with him and writes his goals on the windshield of a car or other creative places.

An athlete writes down his goals while traveling to Greece in order to spark inspiration and create positive habits, which allow his goals to become a reality

See It. Sense It. Savor It.

Posting written goals in a place where they can be *seen* every day, such as on a bathroom mirror, in a training journal, or inside the door of a locker, helps an individual to remain accountable, passionate, and purposeful. It's a friendly reminder of where to head for the day, week, and year. And at the end of the day it can be a helpful reminder to ask, "What did I do to help achieve my goal today?"

After seeing the goal, it is important to *sense it*. Focus on the emotions and bodily sensations of achieving the goal every day. Let the positive thoughts, feelings, smells, and sights fill your body and affect you on a visceral level. Then, *savor it*. Absorbing these good feelings releases dopamine, a neurotransmitter associated with motivation and emotions, and strengthens the neural pathways associated with forming new habits thus bringing you closer to your dreams, goals, and desires.

Rewards to Reinforce

To achieve the biggest dreams and boldest goals, it's important to reinforce behaviors. Why? Because new habits are difficult to form. Building these new habits also sets the stage for other small wins. Seeing small victories creates a pattern that convinces us that bigger achievements are within reach (Amabile & Kramer, 2011; Reay, Golden-Biddle, & Germann, 2006). Yet, a common hurdle in goal setting is we easily forget about the little steps and small victories in our journey to success.

Taking a moment to celebrate the small steps reinforces the excitement of reaching for a goal and supports the sustained motivation required to accomplish long-term goals. Celebrating the achievement of our processes goals on a daily basis, no matter how big or small, enables us to take another motivating step toward the goal. When we celebrate, our brain releases dopamine and instills a feeling of pleasure and this strongly reinforces the initial action or behavior. If we associate actions with pain, suffering, or deprivation, then we are likely to quit reaching for a goal because we naturally want to avoid pain—it's in our DNA.

Choosing process goals that allow us to *gain pleasure and avoid pain* is a key factor to reinforcing behaviors. An example of this is giving a simple reward or celebrating a small win. As you might recall from Chapter 2, rewards are tricky. Extrinsic rewards may undermine intrinsic motivation; however, rewards can instill intrinsic motivation if they raise perceived control and competence.

Tim Ferriss, an American entrepreneur, public speaker, and author who interviews elite athletes and billionaires to find the best tools to enhance performance, advocates celebrating small wins to reinforce goal achievement. To remain creative and motivated, Ferriss got a big mason jar and labeled it the *Jar of Awesome*. Each night he has a habit of writing something he's thankful for on a piece of paper, folds the paper in half, and puts it in the Jar of Awesome. When he feels down, blocked, or unmotivated, he goes to the Jar of Awesome and reads a few of the pieces of paper. Ferriss describes the pieces of paper as *self-made fortune cookies* that give him a dose of pleasure to reinforce he's doing good work. Consequently, he's inspired to keep moving toward his goals.

Another fun way to reward yourself is to think back to a prize you received as a kid. When I was in third grade, it was a smiley face sticker on a paper plate for learning my times tables. Today, I continue to reward my actions or process goals with a sticker. I place the sticker on my calendar for each day I complete my process goals, one of which is meditating before training to induce more flow-like states to boost performance and enjoyment. Every day I see my calendar and how many stickers are on it. This simple reward instills a sense of control that I'm mastering flow-like states and I'm gaining a belief in my ability to improve performance. The reward also gives me a shot of dopamine, which brings me pleasure because I'm able to see the little things I'm doing to achieve my goal. The sticker reward is a simple reminder that my big dreams are becoming a reality. Using a reward that an individual received as a child (i.e., sticker, pat on the back, gummy bears), is a popular and effective goal achieving technique I teach many of my youth, collegiate, and elite athletes.

Overall, it's vital to pause and celebrate small victories. Recognizing ourselves when a job has been well done, no matter how small or outrageous, helps us see success and keep putting one foot in front of the other. As the adage goes, how do you eat an elephant? One bite at a time.

Revisit, Revisit, Revisit

Goals are never static or fixed. Instead they are dynamic and changing. The best way to achieve a goal is to have a comprehensive plan as to how to set them and scheduled times to revisit them. It's common that we set goals for a New Year's Resolution or at the beginning of the season only to never visit them again. That's why in Figure 3.1 there is place to write the date of when a goal was set as well as a *predetermined check-in date* to revisit the goal. This is a built in reminder to help remain accountable.

Revisiting goals is a time to correct barriers, celebrate successes, and adjust and fine-tune strategies to remain inspired and stay on course. *I recommend asking three simple questions when revisiting and reflecting on goals:*

1. Three Ups: What are three things that went well?
2. Three Downs: What are three targets of improvement?
3. Three How's: What are three ways to improve today or tomorrow?

Another effective way to revisit a long-term goal is to create a personalized 30-day challenge. At the beginning of each month, decide on a process goal that will help you to accomplish your larger outcome goal. Then, *ink it*. Write it on a calendar and place the calendar where it can easily be seen every day (e.g., bathroom mirror, work station). Also, remember to reinforce actions with a simple reward like stickers, a pat on the back, or putting money in a jar. At the end of the day, week, or month, take a few minutes to review and refine goals.

An example of this personalized challenge is illustrated in the following scenario. Recently, I counseled a 42-year-old rock climber, entrepreneur, and dad to help him better manage his anxiety and deal with unexpected challenges in order to achieve his outcome goal of climbing harder grades. Each morning at his bathroom sink, the climber decided on a specific daily goal he wanted to accomplish that was in alignment to his outcome and performance goals. He wrote his action-oriented goal on a sticky note and placed it on the bathroom mirror. In the evening while brushing his teeth, he saw the sticky note and was reminded of his daily goal. If he accomplished his goal, then he threw the sticky note away. Tossing the sticky note in the trash was his reward. If he didn't accomplish the goal, then the sticky note remained on the mirror and acted as a friendly reminder of what he wanted to achieve the next morning.

Invite Compassion

Striving to reach new heights isn't always easy. When revisiting goal strategies, remember to be nice to yourself for having the courage to try new challenges. Research suggests that people who are easy on themselves when achieving their goals have a greater sense of life satisfaction, self-acceptance, and achievement while experiencing fewer symptoms of illness, depression, and anxiety (Mosewich et al., 2013; Neff, 2003). This is important to remember, especially for hard-charging, high-achieving athletes and coaches! So, invite compassion. And ignore perfection. Goal achievement is a byproduct of being nice to yourself.

Competition Goals

This chapter has mainly focused on training goals because athletes spend most of their time at practice, improving technique, and developing strength, endurance, and power. This last section briefly covers how to set competition goals.

Competition goals are created for a game, race, meet, or an all-out performance (i.e., sending or onsighting in rock climbing). Setting a variety of goals for competition is important because it helps to decrease the pressure of winning or having a poor performance. Having different goals means success doesn't solely depend on a single outcome. For example, if the only goal is to win, place in a competition, or outperform a previous attempt, then stress and anxiety increases because these goals are not entirely within an athlete's control. Having a variety of goals better allows an individual to play at his or her peak performance because anxiety is reduced. Sensible goals may include an outcome goal such as winning or placing in a meet as well as a performance and process goals that is within the athlete's control. Examples of competition goals that are within the control of the athlete include: using positive self-talk, pacing appropriately, maintaining optimal technique, and giving full effort for the entire performance (even if it isn't going as intended).

I suggest three goal categories for competition: wishbone, backbone, and funny bone.

The *wishbone goal* is an end goal to test learning. It is a goal that may be able to be accomplished, but it's definitely not a given. In setting wishbone goals ask yourself: "What would feel amazing to accomplish? What gets me fired up?" The wishbone goal can be something just outside of your comfort zone or might even be a secret goal where you don't put a limit on what can be achieved. For example, research pioneer and elite sport psychologist Keith Henschen shares a personal story about goal setting. During his earlier years playing basketball, Henschen set a goal to make 50 points in one game. In the first half of the game, Henschen made 48 points! Guess how many points he made in the second half? He made two points. Henschen accomplished his goal of 50 points; however, he put on upper limit on his goal. Thus, the lesson in goal setting was to think of a wishbone or outcome goal as something that is just outside of your perceived capability *or beyond*. You never know what you might achieve.

The wishbone goal is an outcome goal to test learning whereas the *backbone goal* is a process goal to execute the behaviors that are needed to achieve consistent results. The backbone goal refers to the *actions that must be taken just prior to or during the competition* to improve the outcome. Examples of backbone goals include: executing a pre-performance routine, quickly recognizing and reframing a negative thought with a positive belief, going out at a predetermined pace, or breathing deeply during a difficult move in a routine. The problem with backbone goals is that they are hard to prioritize. But, athletes who focus on backbone goals usually feel more in control, which boosts confidence, increases satisfaction, and decreases worry about performing under pressure.

Lastly, the *funny bone* refers to remembering the underlying love of a sport. The funny bone is a goal that is completely within the control of the athlete. My funny bone goal is do my sport with *grace*. For example, while running a race or scaling a rock wall, *grace* means to move and flow with integrity, style, and joy. Another example of a funny bone goal comes from one of my ultrarunner clients. Running 100 miles over mountainous terrain isn't always pretty, so this ultrarunner's funny bone goal is to *keep it sexy*. An Olympian cross country skier once shared with me that she would tell herself that she was going to race so fast that they would have to gender test her. This self-talk was her funny bone goal and made racing feel more light-hearted.

Mainly, a funny bone goal is anything that puts a smile on your face and intrinsically motivates you to pursue excellence. Unfortunately, the funny bone is hard to measure. It's quantifiable from the joy or elation received from the experience, which only can be measured on an individual basis.

Ultrarunner, sports medicine doctor, and mom, Sarah Vlach, remembers her competition goals and mental training skills at an aid station and finishes second in The Bear 100-mile Endurance Run

Ultimately, goal setting takes practice. Athletes can make a wish, but if they do nothing about it then the wish isn't likely to come true. By following the tips and tools in this chapter, you are now ready to set and track personal goals as well as help others with their journey to success. Don't be afraid to experiment with your goals and don't procrastinate making your goals. A good goal today is better than a great goal tomorrow. A final thought from German writer and artist Johann Wolfgang von Goethe, *"Whatever you can do or dream you can do, begin it. Boldness has genius, power, and magic in it. Begin it now."* The next chapter covers another central tenant to champion thinking: performing under pressure.

Summary

- Despite the comprehensive body of research highlighting the performance-enhancing properties of goal setting, most individuals do not set appropriate goals and as a result do not reap the potential benefits.
- Goal setting is defined as "attaining a specific standard of proficiency on a task, usually with a specified time limit" (Locke et al., 1981, p. 126).
- Sport psychology defines goals broadly as: outcome, performance, and process. Outcome goals refer to the end result or a desired target, such as winning a local 5-km race. Performance goals refer to an athlete's personal achievements, such as decreasing 5-km race time by 30 seconds. Process goals refer to specific actions, skills, and strategies to perform satisfactorily, such as performing running drills three times a week in an effort to improve running economy. Each type of goal contributes to success in sports but most athletes neglect to prioritize the small but essential, daily process goals.
- The mnemonic S.M.A.R.T. is a guide to setting effective goals. S.M.A.R.T. stands for specific, measureable, action-oriented, realistic, and timely.
- Other key element in attaining goals include: creating a strong social support system (ABS), putting goals onto paper and posting goals in a visible area, daily review of goals, celebrating the small achievements with simple rewards, revisiting and fine-tuning goals to stay on course, and remembering to give gratitude to yourself and others for trying.

References

Adie, J. W., Duda, J. L., & Ntoumanis, N. (2008). Achievement goals, competition appraisals, and the psychological and emotional welfare of sport participants. *Journal of Sport and Exercise Psychology, 30*(3), 302–322.

Amabile, T. M., & Kramer, S. J. (2011). The power of small wins. *Harvard Business Review, 89*(5), 70–80.

Burton, D. (1989). Winning isn't everything: Examining the impact of performance goals on collegiate swimmers' cognitions and performance. *Sport Psychologist, 3*(2), 105–132.

Burton, D., & Raedeke, T. D. (2008). Goal Setting. In *Sport Psychology for Coaches* (pp. 51–66). Champaign, IL: Human Kinetics.

Burton, D., & Weiss, C. (2008). The Jekyll/Hyde nature of goals: Fine-tuning a performance-based goal-setting model for promoting sport success. In T.S. Horn (ed.), *Advances in sport psychology* (3rd ed.). Champaign, IL: Human Kinetics.

Filby, W. C., Maynard, I. W., & Graydon, J. K. (1999). The effect of multiple-goal strategies on performance outcomes in training and competition. *Journal of Applied Sport Psychology, 11*(2), 230–246.

Helmstetter, S. (1990). *What to say when you talk to yourself.* Simon and Schuster.

Jones, G., & Hanton, S. (1996). Interpretation of competitive anxiety symptoms and goal attainment expectancies. *Journal of Sport and Exercise Psychology, 18,* 144–157.

Kyllo, L. B., & Landers, D. M. (1995). Goal setting in sport and exercise: A research synthesis to resolve the controversy. *Journal of Sport and Exercise Psychology, 17*(2), 117–137.

Locke, E.A. (1996). Motivation through conscious goal setting. *Applied and Preventative Psychology,* 5, 117–124.

Locke, E. A., Shaw, K. N., Saari, L. M., & Latham, G. P. (1981). Goal setting and task performance, 1969–1980. *Psychology Bulletin, 90,* 125–152.

Mosewich, A. D., Crocker, P. R., Kowalski, K. C., & DeLongis, A. (2013). Applying self-compassion in sport: an intervention with women athletes. *Journal of sport & exercise psychology, 35*(5), 514–524.

Neff, K. (2003). Self-compassion: An alternative conceptualization of a healthy attitude toward oneself. *Self and identity, 2*(2), 85–101.

Nicholls, A. R., Perry, J. L., & Calmeiro, L. (2014). Precompetitive achievement goals, stress appraisals, emotions, and coping among athletes. *Journal of Sport and Exercise Psychology, 36*(5), 433–445.

Oettingen, G. (2012). Future thought and behaviour change. *European review of social psychology, 23*(1), 1–63.

Oettingen, G. (2015). *Rethinking positive thinking: Inside the new science of motivation.* Current.

Reay, T., Golden-Biddle, K., & Germann, K. (2006). Legitimizing a new role: Small wins and microprocesses of change. *Academy of Management Journal, 49*(5), 977–998.

Tamminen, K. A., Crocker, P. R., McEwen, C. E., Resende, R., & Alberquerque, A. (2014). Emotional experiences and coping in sport: How to promote positive adaptational outcomes in sport. *Positive human functioning from a multidimensional perspective: Promoting stress adaptation, 1,* 143–162.

Vernacchia, R. A. (2003). Living your dream: Goal attainment. In R. A. Vernacchia (eds.), *Inner Strength: The Mental Dynamics of Athletic Performance* (pp. 85–101). Palo Alto, CA: Warde Publishers.

Weinberg, R., & Butt, J. (2014). Goal-setting and sport performance. *Routledge Companion to Sport and Exercise Psychology: Global Perspectives and Fundamental Concepts*, 343–355.

Weinberg, R. S., & Gould, D. (2014). *Foundations of Sport and Exercise Psychology, 6E*. Human Kinetics.

Weiner, B. (1985). An attribution theory of achievement motivation and emotion. *Psychological Review, 92,* 548–573.

CHAPTER 4

Performing Under Pressure: From Stress to Success

"The only pressure I'm under is the pressure I've put on myself."
—Mark Messier, 25-year NHL veteran.

When performance matters, it's common for athletes to feel under pressure. The heart races, respiratory rate increases, and focus narrows in to the task ahead. How an athlete interprets the physical and mental effects of pressure can change how they think and feel and ultimately how they perform. Athletes often discuss among each other and with their coaches as to how to best manage nerves and worries prior to competition. Because of the prevalence of and potentially profound effects on physical and mental abilities, performance anxiety is the most commonly studied component in sport psychology.

The secret of performing under pressure is not about getting rid of the butterflies, but allowing them to fly in proper formation.

The word *butterflies* is often used to describe feelings of anxiety, stress, and arousal. Although these words are used interchangeably in sports, they have different meanings. This chapter focuses on the nature of these concepts, how they help and hinder performance, and tools to self-regulate so an athlete can perform optimally under pressure.

Anxiety

Anxiety is a negative emotional state of worry, nervousness, or unease about an uncertain outcome (Spielberger, 1966). *Anxiety has two main elements:*

- *Cognitive Anxiety*: The psychological element that refers to the degree to which one worries, experiences self-doubt, feels overwhelmed, or has the inability to concentrate.

- *Somatic Anxiety*: The physiological element that refers to the degree of perceived changes in bodily sensations, such as shortness of breath, sweating, dry mouth, need to urinate, or muscle tension.

Anxiety is not necessarily the actual change in one's mental or physical status. Rather it is the *perception* of these changes and how an individual interprets the butterflies in their stomach or the worry in their mind. Anxious athletes view these signs and symptoms as negative and, thus, it impairs performance. Anxious athletes might say, "I'm scared," "I'm nervous," or "I'm not good enough."

One way to combat anxiety is to *unhook* from negative thoughts, feelings, and experiences (Gardner & Moore, 2004; Hayes & Ciarrochi, 2015). The mind is designed to notice, judge, explain, and compare. Thinking and feeling becomes problematic when an athlete gets caught up in unrealistic negative thoughts and emotions and believes them to be the ultimate truth.

The aim of unhooking is to stop the automatic process of assessing, judging, and predicting and start seeing thoughts and feelings for what they are—just thoughts and feelings, not defining characteristics of who we are or definitive outcomes of a future performance. Unhooking de-emphasizes the content of thoughts so that athletes are freed to perform despite the presence of negative thoughts, feelings, and experiences (O'Connor, 2010).

Unhooking is only possible through self-awareness. We do this by noticing or paying attention to thoughts and feelings from an objective vantage point. Then, we let go. By letting go of these intrusive thoughts and feelings, rather than hooking on to them, it is possible to reduce their negative impact. It's like a juggler who catches and releases a ball. The ball is the negative thought, feeling, or experience. Just as the juggler must notice the balls, one must notice the thoughts, feelings, and experiences and then, let go. The goal isn't to suppress, control, or get rid of the negative experience, rather the goal is to separate from it—or gain distance from it and its consuming grip. By doing so it is possible to reduce and eliminate the negative experience and its undesirable impact on functioning and performance.

Mental Exercise: Unhook from Negative Thoughts

The following is an exercise to help you unhook from anxiety. Pick a word or feeling that describes your anxiety, such as nervous. Repeat the word *nervous* out loud for 30 seconds. Simply notice what happens. What feelings, thoughts, and sensations arise? Can you see the word for what it truly is—a meaningless sound? By repeating the word *nervous*, the significance of the word diminishes and the word loses the grip it has over you because you are not buying into the content. This frees you to perform despite the presence of intrusive thoughts because you have marginalized the importance of the negative construct.

Stress

Stress is an imbalance between task demands, either mental or physical, and one's perceived ability to respond to those task demands. *Examples of task demands include*: increases in training volume, deadlines at work, taking a final exam, or performing optimally in a competition. Stress results when the demands exceed what we *think* we are capable of doing.

A *stressed* athlete, coach, musician, or surgeon sees obstacles or task demands as *threats*. A *successful* athlete, coach, musician, or surgeon see those same obstacles and task demands as healthy or desirable *challenges*. According to researcher and psychologist Kelly McGonigal (2016), "If you believe that the demands of the situation exceed your resources, you will have a threat response. But if you believe you have the resources to succeed, you will have a challenge response."

Both a threat response and a challenge response activate the flight-or-flight stress system. This spikes adrenaline, heart rate, and muscle tension. Contrary to what you might believe, *top performers* aren't physiologically calmer under pressure; rather, they have a *stronger challenge response* (McGonigal, 2016).

This slight shift in one's mindset, seeing a stressful task as a *challenge* rather than a threat, makes a huge difference. Why? The challenge response releases a different ratio of stress hormones, such as higher levels of DHEA—a renewing and recovery hormone. As a result, the challenge response allows performers to access their mental and physical resources, which increases confidence and concentration. Performers feel focused but not fearful. Consequently, performance improves.

Mental Exercise: Stress to Success

Making the move from *stress to success* means calling on your resources. To decrease stress and increase the challenge response, consider these two options:

- Option one: Reduce the task demand, such as decreasing training volume or extending a deadline.
- Option two: Increase your resources or abilities, such as reframing your perception of the situation so it becomes a healthy challenge, improve time management, or hire a sport psychology coach to refine your coping skills.

Arousal

To define arousal, first take a moment to think about what the word arousal means. *Arousal* means to be active, attentive, or excited. Unlike anxiety and stress which are associated with negative feelings, the term arousal is neutral. Because arousal is not associated with good or bad, it's the term used in sport psychology to describe performance anxiety or stress. When athletes are feeling butterflies in their stomach or worrying about how they will perform, using the term arousal, as opposed to anxiety, can give athletes a new perspective regarding these feelings.

Like anxiety, arousal has both psychological and physiological elements. The unscientific way I use to describe arousal to my clients is: *the level of buzz or excitement you feel in both your mind and body*. This level of buzz varies on a continuum of deep sleep (i.e., sleepy cat) to intense excitement (i.e., frenzied fan) (see Figure 4.1).

Arousal is simply a way for an athlete to navigate energy. In sports, arousal activates the mind and body to prepare for intense activity. Throughout a typical day, arousal varies depending on physical and mental requirements. For instance, think about reading this book. How much

Figure 4.1 Arousal Continuum

energy do you have in your body and your mind right now? Where would you put yourself on the arousal continuum? Some situations require low arousal, like reading this book. Whereas getting ready for a competition involves a higher level of arousal. To perform optimally, it's crucial for each person to understand his or her appropriate arousal level for each unique situation (Gould & Krane, 1992; Martens, Vealey, & Burton, 1990). Determining an athlete's level of buzz during competition is an easy first step to understanding how to achieve an optimal level of arousal while under pressure. See the following mental exercise to learn how I help athletes measure their arousal levels.

Mental Exercise: What's Your Level of Buzz?

To gauge an athlete's general level of arousal in training or competition, introduce him or her to the arousal continuum (Figure 4.1) and ask the following questions:

- When you perform your best where is your level of buzz?
- When you perform poorly where is your level of buzz?
- Do you feel the buzz more in your body or more in your mind?
- What strategies do you use to stay in your optimal level of buzz and perform your best?

Recognize to Optimize

Understanding arousal is important so athletes don't become overly aroused and psych themselves out or underaroused and become too relaxed and bored. Either situation results in an inappropriate amount of stress and an athlete will likely not perform to his or her potential. Awareness of one's personal optimal level of arousal is key to peak performance.

In gaining awareness, first it is important to acknowledge and accept that the butterflies in the stomach, sweaty palms, and dry mouth are normal signs of getting ready for an important speech, test, or competition. The body is simply preparing for a *challenge*. As Olympic decathlon gold medalist, Daly Thompson, says: "I love the pressure. I just look forward to it."

Second, for each athlete there is a unique optimal arousal zone. Among athletes, this optimal level of arousal may be displayed outwardly in different manners. For example, a yawning athlete may not appear to care about competition, but the yawn is a way to release tension from being too amped up (Patel, Omar, & Terry, 2010). In addition to understanding one's pre-competition optimal arousal zone, it is essential to know how to best manage fluctuating arousal levels throughout a competition so an athlete can *stay in the zone*. It is important to note that any new strategies used to alter arousal must be practiced in training before incorporating them into a pre-competition routine.

In this next section, we dive into how to find one's personal *optimal arousal zone*. The first step in determining one's optimal arousal zone is to understand both ends of the arousal continuum—overarousal and underarousal.

An athlete managing an ideal arousal level for a maximum weightlift. (PC: Kisa Koenig)

How Overarousal and Underarousal Impacts Performance

If being *in the zone* is a state where an athlete successfully manages energy, channels focus, and feels strong, centered and ready for action, then what does it mean to be overaroused? What does it mean to be under-aroused? And what happens to performance when an athlete is over- or underaroused?

Overarousal is when energy is too high. When overaroused, the athlete is amped up and possibly feels psyched out. According to sport psychology researchers (Burton & Raedeke, 2008; Weinberg & Gould, 2014), performance declines because the athlete experiences challenges in three primary areas: (1) excessive muscle tension, (2) attentional problems, and (3) motor program disruptions.

First, *excessive muscle tension*. Excessive muscle tension leads to awkward movements, limits range of motion, and drains energy, thus, leading to fatigue. Second, overarousal leads to a *narrowing of attention*. When attention overly constricts, the athlete does not pick up on task-relevant cues needed to accurately assess a play, such as reading a defensive tactic or seeing a foot hold while rock climbing. This lack of attention may decrease an athlete's ability to shift focus quickly and make appropriate decisions, thus decreasing performance.

Third, overarousal may also cause problems with an athlete's *motor program*. A once automatic, fluid skill, like swinging a tennis racket, can easily become clumsy when the mind and body are buzzing. When an athlete becomes overaroused, there is a tendency to overanalyze technique, which interrupts muscle memory programming. This process is commonly called *paralysis by analysis*. The muscle memory program for a movement, such as a tennis serve, is a single blueprint that's been created through years of practice but this program becomes less fluid and breaks down into a series of individual steps when one becomes too nervous or thinks too much. Over analysis derails the automatic motor program and, thus, disrupts the natural, instinctive flow of the movement, this increases the risk of movement interruptions and errors. I think using an *analogy of kissing* brings home this point.

Mental Exercise: Paralysis by Analysis via Kissing Analogy

Imagine you were about to kiss your significant other on the lips or kiss your furry pet on the top of the head. Before leaning in for a smooch, you begin pondering on how far to tilt your head, how fast to lean in, and how much you should pucker your lips. If you're analyzing each detail of the kiss, how would the kiss feel? The kiss would probably feel awkward because you already know how to kiss from years of kissing experience. Because you've disrupted the motor program by breaking down each step, the kiss feels strange. The same is true in athletic skills like kicking a ball or skiing down a mountain. When it comes to optimal performance, we must trust our training (i.e., motor program) and let it happen—rather than force it to happen.

Now let's shift gears to the other end of the spectrum—underarousal. *Underarousal* is when energy is too low. When underaroused, an athlete feels bored, too relaxed, and has too broad of a focus (i.e., paying attention to the crowd vs. the game or task). Performance dips because the body is ill-prepared to meet the demands of the situation. When faced with a challenging situation the body prepares for action with the help of the nervous system. The nervous system releases the hormones adrenaline, noradrenaline, and cortisol into the bloodstream. This rush of hormones helps to sharpen attention and readies the body to meet the demands of the task. The cardiovascular system diverts blood flow away from the digestive system to the working muscles to supply additional oxygen and nutrients, which in turn increases an individual's ability to produce force and achieve high velocities. When arousal is too low, the brain doesn't perceive a challenge. Consequently, the nervous system does not release the necessary hormones to produce the physiological changes required for optimal performance. Golf great Jack Nicklaus speaks to the relationship between lack of nerves (underarousal) and performance:

> *"I don't know how you play well unless you're nervous. Nowadays I don't get nervous unless I'm in a major and in position to win. If I could only learn to concentrate when I'm not nervous, so I could get in position to win, then I'd be fine"* (Rotella & Cullen, 1995).

When underaroused (i.e., too relaxed, bored) performance plummets because the mind and body are not prepared to meet the demands of the situation. Performance also suffers when overaroused (i.e., too amped, overly excited) because an athlete likely carries too much muscle tension, becomes too focused, and thinks too much, which hinders the ability to use skills and strengths optimally.

To perform optimally it is critical to find the arousal sweet spot. This sweet spot raises stress levels enough to play at one's best without getting too amped up. Thus, the sweet spot evokes the right amount of physiological changes to achieve excellence and perform to one's unique potential. The next section focuses on how to find that sweet spot.

Finding the Zone of Optimal Functioning

The trick to finding the *arousal sweet spot* is to be fully aware of one's personal stress and energy patterns and manage these feelings and behaviors before entering into a state of overarousal or underarousal. For instance, it's common for an athlete to not recognize mounting stress. Athletes often ignore the warning signs of excessive muscle tension, narrowing of focus, and shortness of breath until they are so stressed that the feelings become too difficult to manage. A state of overarousal builds gradually. If an athlete is aware of the signs and symptoms of overarousal, it can be managed or avoided.

In order to best understand arousal and performance, the following important concepts will be discussed: (1) individualized zone of optimal functioning model, (2) factors related to optimal functioning, and (3) how to assess one's range of optimal functioning and bring awareness to the early signs of overarousal and underarousal as a means to refocus energy and improve performance.

Individualized Zone of Optimal Functioning Model

There are over 50 years of sport psychology research regarding the relationship between arousal and performance. Some related theories include: The Drive Theory (Spence & Spence, 1966), The Inverted-U Hypothesis (Landers & Arent, 2001), and The Catastrophe Model (Hardy, 1990). I recommend athletes, coaches, and practitioners refer to Hanin's (2000) *individualized zone of optimal functioning* theory (IZOF) for a detailed assessment of the optimal arousal zone.

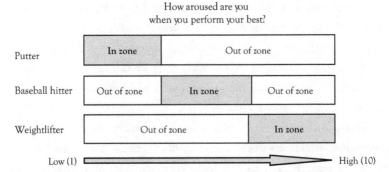

Figure 4.2 Hanin (2000) Individualized Zone of Optimally Functioning

IZOF hypothesizes that when athletes are able to interpret emotions and energy levels within an appropriate time frame they are able to regulate their mental state to facilitate optimal performance. In the IZOF model, each athlete functions at an optimal level that occurs within a bandwidth, or a range, rather than at a single point. Arousal levels within the athlete's designated bandwidth coincide with optimal performance. When outside of this range, the athlete is out of the zone of optimal functioning, which relates to decreased performances (see Figure 4.2).

Some athletes perform best under low levels of arousal, some in the midrange, and others under high arousal. This variation is unique to the personality of the athlete as well as the nature of the sport. For example, putting in golf, a skill that needs great accuracy and sharp focus, typically requires the athlete to have a lower level of arousal to perform optimally. On the other end of the spectrum, a weightlifter performs a skill that demands great strength and power, and therefore, tends to require a higher level of arousal. A baseball hitter's optimal level of arousal likely falls in between putting and weightlifting due to the need for both accuracy and power (see Figure 4.2).

Factors Related to Optimal Functioning: Personality Types and Situations

Many factors contribute to an athlete's zone of optimally functioning. For example, an extroverted personality may perform best when surrounded by friends, whereas an introverted athlete may need a long, quiet warm-up to reach his or her optimal zone of functioning. An example of an extrovert finding the zone of optimal functioning before competition is Tristan Gale, an American skeleton racer and inaugural women's skeleton Olympic gold medalist. Skeleton is a race where competitors get on a small sled, face down, head first, and go around a curvy, frozen track at about 80 mph or more. A few years ago, I was invited to watch Gale compete in Park City, UT. Unlike her other competitors, I observed Gale talking, laughing, and joking with family and friends up until the announcer broadcasted that it was her turn to race. Gale found that surrounding herself with familiar faces immediately before competing allowed her to manage her arousal level, perform her best, and become a world class athlete. Hence, it is key that each athlete understands what works best on an individual basis.

Regardless of age, ability level, or activity, managing one's arousal level is key to finding optimum performance in any adventure

An athlete's zone of optimal functioning also changes depending on the task. Endurance sports like mountain biking and cross-country skiing, may involve brief periods of high arousal but overall the sport requires managing a low level of arousal in order to maintain energy and good form. An event like golf, requires the skill of turning up arousal to tee off and turning down arousal between shots in order to avoid mental fatigue. All in all, athletes must regulate and fine-tune their arousal to meet the demands of the task and their innate personality type.

Assessing Optimal Arousal Levels

Previously discussed was how arousal impacts performance, the significance of regulating arousal to meet task demands, and different factors that contribute to an athlete's ideal arousal level. The next step is learning how to assess an athlete's zone of optimal functioning. According to leading sport psychology researchers and practitioners (Gould & Krane, 1992; Weinberg & Gould, 2014), one of the most effective ways to help athletes achieve peak performance is to increase their *awareness* of how arousal-related emotions can lead to high levels of performance. To become more aware of one's personal optimal level of arousal, complete (or have the athlete complete) the following mental training exercise.

Mental Training Exercise: Assess Your Optimal Arousal Level

- What was your arousal level when you performed at your best? Describe it in detail.
- What was your arousal level when you performed at your worst? Describe in detail.
- Describe a time when your arousal and performance fluctuated depending on what you were thinking and feeling? What were the ways you dealt with these experiences?
- Explain how you think your personality influences your ideal arousal level?
- Explain how you think the nature of your sport affects your arousal level?

To further assist an athlete in identifying their ideal arousal level or IZOF, have them rate their optimal bandwidth on the 1 to 10 arousal continuum (see Figure 4.1), one represents low arousal (too low and associated with poor performance) and 10 represents high arousal (too high and associated with poor performance). For example, have the athlete think back to one of their best performances. A time where they were focused, centered, and on top of their game. Ask them to recall what their arousal level was on the 1 to 10 arousal continuum. For instance, an athlete might recall an optimal arousal level as a 4 or between a 3 and a 5 on a scale of 1 to 10.

Continue developing and fine-tuning an optimal individual arousal level by taking the discussion to practice. For the next week (3 to 5 days), at the end of practice identify a time during practice when arousal level was low, a time when it was high, and a time it was optimal. Try to have the athlete link their arousal level to their level of performance then make the connection to their arousal bandwidth that corresponds with optimal performance (i.e., 3 to 5). After you determine the athlete's bandwidth, discuss one way they can regulate their arousal level in an effort to spend 1 percent more time within that bandwidth during the next practice.

During the following week of practice, take a few 30-second breaks during practice to have athletes individually assess their arousal level. Give each athlete a notecard with the arousal continuum scale of 1 to 10. Mark one on the left side of the note card and 10 is on the right side. At predetermined checkpoints, have athletes mark their arousal level on the notecard as well as how they think they are performing. At the end of every practice, each athlete should view his or her patterns of over-arousal, underarousal, or optimal arousal and discuss their results with teammates and coaches. This activity not only brings awareness to personal arousal level patterns but it can also spark a discussion regarding why there is deviation from optimal arousal zones. Understanding and self-monitoring these deviations can help athletes determine strategies to stay in the zone.

If you're seeking more tools and techniques to stay in the zone of optimal functioning, look no further. The next chapter teaches specific relaxation and energization skills to manage arousal and achieve peak performance.

Summary

- It's common to feel pressure, but inappropriately interpreting this pressure can have a negative impact on performance.
- Pressure in sports is described as anxiety, stress, and arousal. Although these words are often used interchangeably, within the context of sport psychology, each has a different meaning.
- Anxiety is a negative emotional state, such as worry, nervousness, or unease about an uncertain outcome. One technique to overcome anxiety is to unhook from these thoughts, feelings, and experiences. By paying attention to them and letting them come and go, rather than being attached to them, an athlete can reduce anxiety's negative impact.
- Stress is an imbalance between the task demands (e.g., increased training volume, meeting a work deadline, performing well at a major event or final examinations) and one's perceived ability to respond to that demand. We stress over the demands placed on us because what we are asked to do exceeds what we think we are capable of doing. A way to navigate stress is to manage the task demands (e.g., adjusting training schedules) or to increase ability (e.g., improving time management, gaining strength).
- Arousal means to excite. Overarousal is when energy is too high, whereas underarousal is when energy is too low, both are detrimental to performance.
- The individualized zone of optimal functioning (IZOF) model is an easy-to-use tool to understand optimal arousal zones. In IZOF, each athlete functions at an optimal level. This optimal level is not a single point, rather it is within a bandwidth. Some athletes perform best under low levels of arousal, some in the midrange, and others under high arousal.
- Personality types (introverts vs. extroverts) and situations (endurance vs. power sports) also influence an athlete's zone of optimal functioning.
- Self-awareness is key for each performer to understand his or her optimal zone of functioning and to consistently perform at a high level.

References

Burton, D., & Raedeke, T. D. (2008). Energy Management. In *Sport Psychology for Coaches* (pp. 139–154). Champaign, IL: Human Kinetics.

Gardner, F. L., & Moore, Z. E. (2004). A Mindfulness-Acceptance-Commitment-Based approach to athletic performance enhancement: Theoretical considerations. *Behavior Therapy, 35*, 707–723.

Gould, D., & Krane, V. (1992). The arousal-athletic performance relationship: Current status and future directions. In T.S. Horn (ed.), *Advances in Sport Psychology* (pp. 119–142). Champaign: Human Kinetics.

Hanin, Y. I. (2000). Individual zones of optimal functioning (IZOF) model: Emotion-performance relationship in sport. In Y.I. Hanin (ed.), *Emotions in sport* (pp. 65–89). Champaign, IL: Human Kinetics.

Hardy, L. (1990). A catastrophe model of performance in sport. In G. Jones & L. Harder (eds.), *Stress and performance in sport* (pp. 81–106). Chichester, UK: Wiley.

Hayes, L., & Ciarrochi, J. (2015). Using acceptance and commitment therapy to help young people develop and grow to their full potential. In *Promoting Psychological Well-Being in Children and Families* (pp. 102–122). UK: Palgrave Macmillan.

Landers, D. M., & Arent, S. M. (2001). Physical activity and mental health. In R. Singer, H. Hausenblas, & C. Janelle (eds.), *Handbook of sport psychology* (2nd ed., pp. 740–765). New York: Wiley.

Martens, R., Vealey, R. S., & Burton, D. (1990). *Competitive anxiety in sports*. Champaign: Human Kinetics.

McGonigal, K. (2016). *The upside of stress: Why stress is good for you, and how to get good at it*. Penguin.

O'Connor, E. (2010). Defusion: When positive thinking doesn't work. *Signature Sport Psychology Techniques That Link Theory and Practice Symposium*.

Patel, D. R., Omar, H., & Terry, M. (2010). Sport-related performance anxiety in young female athletes. *Journal of Pediatric and Adolescent Gynecology, 23*(6), 325–335.

Rotella, R., & Cullen, R. (1995). *Golf is not a game of perfect*. New York: Simon & Schuster.

Spence, J. T., & Spence, K. W. (1966). The motivational components of manifest anxiety: Drive and drive stimuli. In C.D. Spielberger (ed.), *Anxiety and behavior*. (pp. 291–326). New York: Academic Press.

Spielberger, C. D. (1966). Theory and research on anxiety. In C.D. Spielberger (ed.), *Anxiety and behavior* (pp. 3–22). New York: Academic Press.

Weinberg, R. S., & Gould, D. (2014). Arousal regulation. In *Foundations of Sport and Exercise Psychology, 6E* (pp. 273–294). Champaign, IL: Human Kinetics.

CHAPTER 5

Play at Your Peak: Developing Relaxation and Energization Strategies

The athlete who is in championship form has a quiet place in himself. And it's out of that his action comes. If he's all in the action field, he's not performing properly. There's a center out of which you act; in dance this is true, too. There's a center that has to be known and held. It's quite physically recognized by the person. But unless this center has been found, you're torn apart. Tension comes.
—Joseph Campbell, American mythologist, writer and lecturer

Athletes, coaches, public speakers, and other professionals who perform at a high level recognize the importance of calming down or psyching up if they want to find the arousal sweet spot and perform well. Yet, many people don't know how to relax or energize themselves because they've never been taught the skills. This chapter gives examples regarding the use and application of relaxation and energization skills to manage arousal, become anchored in the present moment, and perform in the zone of optimal functioning.

Relax to Achieve the Max

Relaxation evokes mental and physical responses which decrease the detrimental effects of being overaroused, stressed, or anxious. When feeling too amped up, the natural tendency is to hold the breath which, in turn, increases muscle tension. This interferes with the smooth, coordinated movements necessary for maximum performance. During relaxation, we breathe deeply which releases unwanted muscle tension, calms the nervous system, and quiets the mind. Thus, the mind and body sync together and become an integrated system. Absorbing oneself in relaxation helps shift thoughts and feelings away from those that are self-sabotaging. When individuals are relaxed, they feel in control and can maximize the skills and strengths needed to reach their full potential. For example, my client Hadley Hammer, a professional big mountain skier, speaks to the importance of a relaxation tool that she now uses to center herself:

> *For me, I use the body scan [sequentially relaxing muscles] because I'm in the pursuit of reconnecting my brain with my body. The body scan lets me focus on single parts of my body. It helps me know what's tight or sore or what feels good. And it helps me let my brain focus on one thing. Disconnect from e-mails, social posts, to-do lists etc, etc. It really helps me bring my mind and body together which are key elements for my skiing.*

There are many effective relaxation techniques that can be used to improve performance. The best relaxation techniques are those that make the athlete feel good, centered, and ready for action. This chapter introduces science-based relaxation skills that I, and the athletes I have worked with, find to be most effective, applicable, and easiest to practice. The skills include: *belly breathing, square breathing, progressive muscle relaxation, and music.*

Fundamentals of Relaxation

Before practicing any relaxation technique it is important to find a quiet, comfortable setting to practice, such as by a babbling brook or in the comfort of one's bedroom.

This next piece is best understood through personal practice; follow the upcoming script to gain a better understanding of relaxation fundamentals.

Mental Exercise: Relaxation 101

Start by focusing on your posture. Good posture is a key ingredient before starting any relaxation technique. Sit on a chair with both feet flat on the floor or lie on your back on the ground. Now, gently close your eyes. Take a moment to sit tall or lengthen your spine with your back comfortably straight; head and spine held in good alignment. Rest your hands on your thighs or by your side. Relax your shoulders by allowing the shoulder blades to lower and rest loosely in the center of your back. At any time during this relaxation exercise, slightly adjust your posture so that you remain relaxed and comfortable. Begin to notice the breath. Breathe easily and comfortably. Every time your mind tries to stray to something else gently, but firmly, bring it back to the point of focus, your breath. After five breaths, gently open your eyes.

Don't worry if you find relaxation techniques difficult. It is normal for the mind to wander. Simply be relaxed—do nothing except sit and breathe. With regular practice, relaxation will become easier and more enjoyable.

Lastly, think of these relaxation exercises as a *metronome*. A metronome is a tool that helps musicians develop a regular, rhythmic beat and is fundamental to mastering music. Like a metronome, breathing, or any relaxation technique can be a powerful tool to consistently and rhythmically connect to that still space within and provide a mechanism to center yourself.

Belly Breathing

Bud Winter, coach of many great Olympic athletes and author of *Relax and Win: Championship Performance in Whatever You Do*, believes that breathing and relaxation are the most widely ignored aspect of athletic performance, yet the most crucial (Winter, 1981). Although breathing is innate, learning to master respiratory rate, rhythm, and depth during stressful situations is a skill that usually needs to be learned and practiced. It's only when an athlete's mind and body are relaxed and working together that *optimal performance is born*.

Belly breathing is a technique intended to help an athlete to manage breathing patterns and improve the ability to relax. When someone is overaroused, they tend to increase respiratory rate but depth of the breath is shallow and the rate of the breath is fast, all of which are less effective means of transporting oxygen. When calm and centered we tend to breathe slowly and deeply, which is a more effective means of transporting oxygen. Belly breathing helps to increase the depth of the breath and slow an exaggerated respiratory rate so oxygen perfusion can be maximized and the brain and body can work together to perform in the zone of optimal functioning.

Belly breathing involves filling the lungs from the bottom up. While inhaling, the diaphragm, a thin muscle separating the lungs from the abdominal cavity, moves downward and creates a vacuum. This allows the lungs to fill optimally. Obviously we don't actually fill the stomach (or belly) with air but for the purposes of understanding and *feeling* the technique you can think of belly breathing as similar to filling a vase full of water; the torso is the vase and water fills from the bottom to the top (i.e., from your belly to your ribs and to your upper chest). Filling a vase full of water can be a nice visual while practicing belly breathing.

Mental Exercise: Belly Breathing Script

The first step to belly breathing is noticing the breath. Sitting with good posture, begin by softly inhaling through the nose. During the inhalation, focus on the in-breath and where and how the air travels through your body. Next, slowly exhale out through the mouth. Focus on the out-breath and how the air is released from your body. Breathe easily and comfortably.

Next, place one hand on your belly and the other hand on your chest. Notice as you breathe which hand moves more. Is it the hand over your belly or is it the hand over your chest?

Continue to slowly inhale through your nose. Inhale and feel your belly fill with air. Feel your belly growing in all directions, similar to a balloon expanding. Begin to gently exhale through your mouth letting your belly slowly relax and move back to center. Again, inhale to fill up your belly then feel your breath moving up to the middle portion of your torso and completely fill your rib cage. Feel the rib cage expand out like an accordion. Exhale out through your mouth and gently release the breath back to center. On the next inhale, breathe smoothly into your belly, then into your rib cage and finally feel your breath move just a bit higher as it fills the areas in your chest and shoulders. Without force, feel the breath move easily and effortlessly into the upper areas of your chest—filling the space even under your clavicles. Smoothly exhale through your mouth and release your breath fully. Continue belly breathing for 1 minute or however long you feel comfortable.

The Accelerator and the Brake

To improve relaxation while practicing belly breathing, extend the exhalation. The exhale portion of the breath should be as long as or slightly longer than inhalation because exhalation increases activation of the parasympathetic nervous system.

Breathing is managed by the autonomic nervous system which has two parts: *the sympathetic nervous system and parasympathetic nervous system.* When stressed, anxious, or overaroused, the *sympathetic nervous system* turns on and floods the body with stress hormones. This is known as the *fight or flight stress response.* These stress hormones, like cortisol and adrenaline, ready the mind and body to meet the demands of a situation. But when stress hormones build up, it limits our ability to think clearly and respond appropriately.

On the other hand, the *parasympathetic nervous system* counterbalances the detrimental effects of too many circulating stress hormones. The parasympathetic nervous system releases a key ingredient to support relaxation, a neurochemical called acetylcholine. Acetylcholine slows down heart rate and lowers blood pressure. This system is known as *rest and digest* and is an important mechanism to balance out the fight or flight stress response.

The two parts of the autonomic nervous system can be thought of as an *accelerator* and a *brake* on a car. The accelerator is the sympathetic nervous system, which pushes the pedal to the metal and ramps up the body. The brake is the parasympathetic nervous system, which causes the body to slow down. Using the brake and accelerator improperly may cause the spark plugs to misfire and wastes fuel. The same is true with our brains and bodies—when used incorrectly, the brake (parasympathetic) and accelerator (sympathetic) are out of sync and don't run well. In order to avoid burning out, it's essential to learn how and when to speed up versus slow down.

Since breathing is managed by the autonomic nervous system, focusing on the breath is a simple, effective way to activate relaxation and get the mind and body in sync. The parasympathetic nervous system is activated during exhalation, thus, exhaling as long or up to twice as long as the inhalation helps to balance out the stress response and put on the brakes if necessary. Synchronizing the parts of the autonomic nervous system improves the ability to focus, learn, and reason (Davidson et al., 2003). Therefore, the more deeply one focuses on the breath, the more anchored, calm, and centered they can be; and being composed in the present moment is an essential element to optimizing performance.

Practicing Belly Breathing

Just like physical fitness, it takes time to become mentally fit. With physical training the muscles hypertrophy (i.e., increase tissue volume) because of strategic increases in workload. Using muscles in new ways stimulates muscle growth. This is also true for the brain. Increasing the workload of the brain (e.g., focusing on your breathing, problem solving, etc.), causes one to become mentally fit. This is based on the power of *neuroplasticity*, a term used to describe the brain changes that occur in response to an experience (Davidson & Begley, 2013). By practicing only a few minutes each day, the brain can strengthen the connection between neurons and begin to hardwire skills such as calmness, confidence, and motivation (Draganski et al., 2004; Graham & Hanson, 2013). Eventually, through practice, one is able to call upon these states of relaxation on demand. Simply put, by practicing breathing skills the brain is capable of changing itself, and when needed, entering into a more relaxed state.

To improve this skill, begin practicing belly breathing for 1 minute every day. To help you get started, you can set a timer, use the free app CalmMyBeat, or make and play an audio recording of the script in this book. *Link this new habit* of belly breathing to another habit in order to help you remember to practice. An example of linking a new habit with a habit you do every day might be belly breathing before you eat breakfast or after you brush your teeth. After you feel comfortable practicing belly breathing for 1-minute progress to 2-minutes with a goal of 10 to 20 minutes per day. Belly breathing typically takes 10 weeks of consistent practice to master (Davidson & Begley, 2013).

Composed in the present moment, professional mountain athlete, Sam Elias, uses breathing techniques to optimize performance while rock climbing

Square Breathing

Before the 2013 NBA playoffs, cameras caught a glimpse of LeBron James sitting on the bench with his eyes closed, as George Mumford a sport psychology coach for NBA players writes in his book *The Mindful Athlete* (Mumford, 2015). You'd think that James would be focusing on his opponents or other outside factors, rather, James was focusing within. With all the commotion around him, James was concentrating on his breathing and clearing a space in his mind so he could get into a flow state and sustain it when he returned to the game.

We've all seen athletes sitting quietly before competition, bringing their attention not to the game ahead but to the present moment. Being aware of breathing is a simple, fundamental technique for finding that calm, centered place within. The most popular centering technique I teach athletes with whom I work is square breathing.

Square breathing is a technique that uses the mind to calm the body. This is a *mind-to-muscle* technique (Martens, 1987) because it helps to focus a racing mind or ease worrying thoughts, which in turn relaxes the body. In pressure-filled situations, if an athlete experiences cognitive anxiety (i.e., feeling buzz or arousal primarily in the mind rather than in the body), then a mind-to-muscle technique works to reduce this psychological arousal and, consequently, aids in relaxing the body. Belly breathing, on the other hand, is a *muscle-to-mind* technique designed to relax the body or muscles, which aids in calming the mind. Muscle-to-mind techniques work primarily to decrease physiological arousal associated with somatic anxiety (i.e., feeling buzz or arousal in the body). Both techniques are beneficial. Experiment with the relaxation exercises in this book and choose the strategy that enables you, your athletes, or your employees to more effectively manage arousal levels and perform better.

Mental Exercise: Square Breathing Script

Begin square breathing by getting into a comfortable seated position in a quiet location. Begin to imagine the shape of a square. It can be big or small. The square can be any color you choose. Notice the four sides of the square. See all four corners. Bring your attention to the top-left corner. From the top-left corner, breathe around the square in a counterclockwise direction.

To breathe around the square, first breathe naturally in and out through your nose. On the next inhalation, easily move your breath from the top-left corner down the left side of the square. Gently pause at the corner. Smoothly exhale across the bottom edge of the square. Briefly pause at the bottom-right corner. Inhale up the right side. Pause at the top corner. Exhale across the top. And pause at the corner to complete the square. Continue to breathe around the square by inhaling on the vertical sides, exhaling on the horizontal lines, and pausing at the corners.

Practice lengthening the inhalation and exhalation to a 4-second count (i.e., 4-4-4-4). Pause at each corner for 1 second as you transition between breaths. Practice this by breathing in for 4 seconds. Pause a moment. Breathe out for 4 seconds, pause, and so on.

With practice, try to lengthen the exhalation for a longer time without straining yourself. Lengthening an exhalation activates your brake, the parasympathetic nervous system, helping you to become more relaxed. For example, try breathing in for 4 seconds, pausing and exhaling out for 8 seconds.

As you continue to breathe in and out around the square, pay attention to the pauses at each corner. The brief pause is the space between your inhalation and exhalation. Become aware of how this spaciousness creates a centering place inside you. Notice how the pauses are naturally peaceful and calming—a place that anchors you in-the-now. It's like the calm eye in the center of a tornado—a place where you may notice the whirlwind around, but you don't feel the commotion or connect to the chaos because you are deeply rooted in your center. I call this *Taming the Tornado*. Continue to breathe around the square, pausing at the corners, for 1 minute on your own.

Navigate the Noise

One of the biggest distractions of the mind is noise. Noise mainly comes from the mental chatter or negative self-talk inside your head as well as outside distractions like the roar of a crowd. Square breathing helps to quiet the noise and relax the mind by bringing awareness back to your breath and focusing on what's in front of you—the present moment. Anecdotally, I think the reason why square breathing is the most popular breathing technique I teach is that most athletes, coaches, teachers, or parents are either unaware of the noise inside their own head or they do not have any tools to navigate the noise. Square breathing gives them a mind-to-muscle tool to become focused and calm the noisy, restless mind. George Mumford shares what Kobe Bryant says about noise and how he gets into the zone:

When you get in the Zone, things just slow down. Everything slows down. You have supreme confidence. When that happens, you really do not try to focus on what's going on (around you) because out there (in the crowd), you could lose it in a second. Everything becomes one noise. You're not paying attention to this or that noise. You have to really try to stay in the present, not let anything break that rhythm. You just stay here. You're kind of locked in.

The effectiveness of square breathing is not just anecdotal. It is also aligned with emerging research. Breathing at certain paces has an impact on heart rate and rhythm, which improves psychophysiological (mind-body) functioning, health, recovery, and performance (Strack & Gervirtz, 2011; Yasuma & Hayano, 2004). Although everyone has a personal optimal pace for breathing, research supports that approximately six breaths per minute is an ideal breathing pace to synchronize your brain and body (Schwartz & Andrasik, 2015). Six breaths per minute is equivalent to a 10-second breath count. Square breathing is a 10-second breath (4-second inhale, 1-second pause, 4-second exhale, and 1-second pause). Thus, the rhythmic pace of square breathing optimally engages both the sympathetic nervous system (fight or flight) and the parasympathetic nervous system (rest and digest). This balanced state improves overall health and performance.

Practicing Square Breathing

Like belly breathing, practice square breathing for 1 minute progressing to 10 to 20 minutes a day. With diligent and regular practice, you will be better at quieting the mind and, thus the body. The more you deliberately practice, the easier it will get.

Progressive Muscle Relaxation

Progressive muscle relaxation (PMR) is a more elaborate skill than the previous breathing techniques. It is an acquired skill that allows athletes to feel or notice muscle tension and, then, let go of that tension (Jacobson, 1938). During a tension cycle, an individual gradually builds up muscle tension to maximally contract a specific muscle group. A tension cycle lasts for 5 to 7 seconds. This is followed by allowing the muscles to completely relax for 20 to 60 seconds. Experiencing a period of tension and a period with a lack of tension, or relaxation, helps an individual learn the difference between tensed and relaxed muscles.

There are two main phases of PMR. The first phase of PMR involves 20 minutes or more of tensing and relaxing specific muscle groups. A sample PMR script can be found in this chapter on page 88. The second phase of PMR consists of attaining deep relaxation in four major muscle groups:

1. Both feet, calves, thighs, and hips
2. Back, stomach, and chest (torso)
3. Both shoulders, arms, and hands
4. Head and neck

After practicing Phase one and Phase two, the relaxation response of PMR can be condensed to a body scan as well as reduced to only a few seconds with the use of a *self-instructed cue*, like *Relax* or *Soft is Strong*. Personally, I've developed the cue word *tranquility*. After practicing 20-minute sessions of PMR for 2 weeks and moving onto relaxing the four major muscle groups for another week, I am now able to use the word *tranquility* when I notice tightness and anxiety building, whether that be being frustrated at the grocery store or preparing to rock climb a hard route. Relaxing with a self-instructed cue is a skill that requires weeks of practice, but with practice one can use PMR to detect and release tensed muscles in a variety of stressful situations. The following Cued Relaxation section provides more details regarding use of a cue word to relax.

Practicing PMR

Practice PMR with the script found on page 88. PMR should be practiced three to five times a week for a minimum of 2 to 3 weeks then at least once a week thereafter. After achieving deep relaxation, progress from using the PMR script to practicing relaxation in the four major muscle groups: (1) both feet, calves, thighs, and hips, (2) back, stomach, and chest (torso), (3) both shoulders, arms, and hands, and (4) head and neck. Practice deep relaxation in the four major muscle three to five times a week for 1 to 2 weeks. With practice, you can eventually bring a rapid relaxation response within one breath.

A similar technique to PMR is the body scan. PMR is tensing and relaxing muscles whereas the body scan is when an athlete is sensing for any unwanted muscle tightness (without tensing the muscle) and, then, relaxes these muscles. The body scan is typically used as part of a pre-performance competition routine. For example, in the quote at the beginning of this chapter Hadley Hammer described how she used the body scan technique before skiing to help her connect her mind and body and perform optimally. Athletes can practice the body scan by using the PMR Phase two format by deeply relaxing the four main muscle groups (i.e., (1) legs and hips, (2) torso, (3) shoulder and arms, and (4) head and neck). Rather than tensing the muscles as in PMR, the body scans each muscle group for any unnecessary muscle tension (some muscle tension is needed for sport) and relaxes that tension.

Mental Exercise: Progressive Muscle Relaxation Script

Progressive muscle relaxation is more elaborate than other breathing techniques and is an acquired skill that incorporates creating muscle tension and letting go of that tension. Initially, this exercise may take 20 minutes or more to complete.

To begin, lie on the floor in a comfortable position and take some long, slow breaths. Don't force your breaths, but simply notice as it gently flows in through your nose and continues down into your belly and lungs. Exhale smoothly through your nose and feel the air naturally leave your body. With this calming breath, gently close your eyes.

During this progressive muscle relaxation, we are going to work each muscle group starting from our toes and work our way to the top of our heads. As we progress through each muscle group, you will first tense the designated muscle for a few seconds and then relax for a few seconds. Tensing muscles is like an accelerator on a car. First you push on the gas pedal and start tensing at 10 mph, then gradually build to 20 mph, 30 mph, and all the way to 100 mph. Remember, the muscle tension (or acceleration) lasts about 5 seconds. After 5 seconds, let go of any muscle tension all at once—relaxing your muscles for about 20 seconds. Don't strain to relax, just let it happen.

The cue to begin tensing muscles is *Tense NOW* or *Go*. The cue to relax tense muscles is *Ok, Relax* or *Let Go*.

We'll begin the progressive muscle relaxation exercise with our feet. Tense the muscles in your feet by curling your toes toward the ground. Curl just your toes and no other body part. Tense NOW (5 seconds). Notice the sensation of tension in the ball of your foot. Ok, relax (20 seconds). As all the tension drains out, feel the spreading sensation of relaxation in the bottoms of your feet.

Now flex your ankles as though you're trying to touch your toes to your shin. Tense NOW (5 seconds). You should feel a lot of tension through your calf, ankle, and foot. Contrast this tension from when you tensed your feet by curling your toes. Ok, relax (20 seconds). Let go of the tension. Relax your muscles as easily and deeply as possible. Let your calves melt into the floor.

Next, turn your attention to your thighs. Tighten these muscles by contracting all of the muscles in your quadriceps and hamstrings. Tense NOW (5 seconds). Try to feel the tension in your thighs only. Remember this tight sensation. Ok, relax (20 seconds). Contrast the tension with feelings of relaxation. Remember that relaxation is merely the absence of tension. Relax as deeply and completely as possible.

In progressive muscle relaxation, it's sometimes helpful for individuals to use visualization. Next time we tense, you may want to imagine a bright red color. As you tense, the muscle is fire hot like an ember. To help you relax the muscle, visualize the ember cooling to a soft yellow or blue.

Next, focus on your buttocks. Squeeze your butt muscles together so tight that you're holding a $100 bill between your cheeks and you don't want me to pull it out. Tense NOW (5 seconds). Imagine a bright red color, it is hot like an ember as you tense the muscle. Remember to only contract your butt muscles and relax every other muscle in your body. Ok, relax your bum (20 seconds). Exhale completely and allow the ember to cool off to a soft yellow—still glowing and warm, yet totally relaxed. Or imagine a watery blue that's fluid, flexible, and tranquil.

Now move to the upper body. Progressively tighten your abdomen as though you're about to get punched in the gut. Tense NOW (5 seconds). You should feel tightness in only your stomach—your shoulders and other muscles remain relaxed. Ok, release the tension by gradually letting it all drain out. Just let it happen (20 seconds). Relax.

We will begin to tense the muscles in both hands and lower arms by making a tight first. Begin to tense, NOW (5 seconds). Feel the tension in the hand, knuckles, and forearm. Ok, relax by simply letting go of the tension (20 seconds). Notice the difference between tension and relaxation. Let all the tension melt away. Your arms and hands feel heavy and warm.

Continue to breathe deeply as we move our attention to our shoulders. To tense your shoulders, shrug your shoulders up toward your ears. Begin shrugging NOW (5 seconds). Ok, release the tension (20 seconds). Replace tension with a feeling of relaxation that soothes every fiber in your muscles. The tightness in your shoulders loosens and releases.

Next, tense the muscles in your neck by trying to pushing your head down to the floor while simultaneously trying to nod. Tense NOW (5 seconds). Feel the slight discomfort. Ok, relax (20 seconds). Drain all the tension from the muscles in your neck. Your neck is soft and smooth.

Turn your attention to the muscles in your face. Tense the muscles in your forehead by raising your eyebrows and also tensing your face muscles by pulling the corners of your mouth back to make a big smile. Tense NOW (5 seconds). Ok, relax (20 seconds). Let go of the muscle tension in your face all at once. We carry a lot of unrealized tension in our face muscles, so let any noticed tightness dissolve away.

Lastly, we are going to tense every muscle in our body. Tense NOW (5 seconds)—feet, calves, thighs, bum, abs, torso, shoulders, arms, hands, and head. And, RELAX. Allow all the muscles in your body go limp (20 seconds). As you breathe slowly and deeply, let all traces of tension leave your body. Currents of tranquility and peace soothe every muscle, every nerve and every fiber in your being.

For a few minutes on your own, begin to scan your body for any place that has residual tension. Wherever you still feel tense, do additional tensing and relaxing. Feel the tension in your body lessen more and more. To ensure you are completely relaxed throughout your entire body, score your total relaxation on a scale of 1 to 10; 1 being totally relaxed and 10 being the most tensed you've ever been. The goal is to be at a 3 or less. If you're not at a 3, continue to scan your body and tense or relax or breathing deeply with total focus on the feelings of relaxation in every part of your body.

During this exercise you may notice a sensation of warmth and heaviness, or you may float and feel light as air. There is no right or wrong way to feel. Go with whatever feelings you have. Simply enjoy the sensation of relaxation.

Now, think of a word that explains how your body feels right now. Say that word to yourself. Begin to say this word silently on each exhale. This word is a self-directed cue meant to strengthen the association between your word and total relaxation in your body. It is a cue to help your body remember this relaxed state. Use this cue word to go deeper and into a more relaxed state.

Before opening your eyes, take several deep breaths and feel energy and alertness flowing back into your body. Stretch your arms and legs. Your body should feel relaxed and your mind should be calm, centered, and ready to focus on the rest of your day. When you're ready, open your eyes and slowly make your way to a seated position. Congratulations on completing this imagery script. I hope you will continue to practice this exercise as a means to help you achieve a clear mind and calm body and play at your peak.

Music to Relax

Music is a technique most athletes use to help them relax, get psyched, or enhance mental focus for better athletic performance. Athletes may feel the rhythm of the music or relate to the lyrics of a favorite song. Either way, music can be used as a trigger to promote relaxation, energization, heightened awareness, and concentration.

To foster relaxation, mental focus, and performance enhancement, music can help in a variety of ways. Examples include: a skier listening to calming music in training to ski with fluidity, a golfer listening to a relaxing playlist before tee-off time to help sync her swing, or an athlete listening to soothing tunes in the car while driving to the training or competition venue.

Music improves performance by *changing brain waves*. The brain is made up of billions of cells called neurons. Neurons use electricity to communicate with each other and the rest of the body. Billions of neurons send signals at the same time generating a large amount of electrical activity in the brain. This activity can be measured with an electroencephalography (EEG).

When you graph the electrical activity in your brain, it creates a brain-wave pattern. The four brain-wave patterns are: beta, alpha, theta, and delta. *Theta and delta* waves are lower frequency waves (0.1 to 8 hertz) that occur during dreaming and dreamless sleep, respectively. Theta waves also occur during deep meditation. *Beta waves*, the highest frequency wave (12+ hertz), occur when we are concentrating, alert, aroused, and slightly stressed. Higher frequency beta waves indicate that we are stressed, anxious, or diseased—not an ideal state to be living, exercising, or competing in.

When we lower the brain-wave frequency to *alpha waves* (8 to 12 hertz), we can focus better, learn more, analyze complex situations, and even be in a state of heightened awareness or *the zone* (Miyachi et al., 2014). Lower frequency alpha waves indicate there is a slightly decreased electrical activity in the brain. This state increases the release of endorphins, norepinephrine, and dopamine—a cocktail of feel-good neurochemicals. Meditations like a mantra, a prayer, or the breathing exercises in this chapter, bring the brain into an alpha state because electrical activity slows down and brain waves stabilize into a relaxed range. This allows for a heightened state of awareness and focus and in turn, improves performance.

Certain music influences brain waves by allowing for a state of relaxed focus. This relaxed state improves learning, analyzing, and heightens awareness. How? The human brain has a tendency to shift its brain-wave frequency toward the frequency of the dominant external stimuli (i.e., music, sound). Brain-wave frequencies sync with the specific frequency of the music or auditory stimuli that is being played (Bood, Nijssen, van der Kamp, & Roerdink, 2013; Schneider, Askew, Abel, & Strüder, 2010). Therefore, using music to promote relaxation, or energization, is best accomplished using specific frequencies.

A research study shows that listening to music of 3-hertz frequency brings the brain into an alpha brain-wave state and this enhances both mood and performance output (Schneider, et al., 2010). Schneider and colleagues (2010) wished to determine whether a frequency of 3-hertz during running is synchronized with different intrinsic (physiological systems: heart rate, brain cortical activity) and extrinsic (music) frequencies. In studying 18 healthy runners, they reported a strong relationship between intrinsic and extrinsic oscillation patterns during outdoor running sessions at different intensities. Data revealed a peak frequency of 2.7 to 2.8 Hz for improved performance in running. They found that runners rated their workouts as pleasurable when voluntarily choosing music that was approximately 3-hertz frequency. During repetitive, endurance-type activities, self-selected, motivational music has been shown to enhance mood, reduce ratings of perceived exertion, improve energy efficiency, and lead to increased work output; however, this music may not be as effective during high-intensity activities with exertion beyond the anaerobic threshold (i.e., lactate threshold) (for review, see Karageorghis & Priest, 2012).

A frequency of 3-hertz is 3 beats per second or 180 beats per minute. If you want a music selection to accompany you in a relaxed, flow state for a self-paced, submaximal exercise, such as long, slow training days in running, biking, or cross country skiing, I recommend downloading music tracks with 180 beats per minute. Also, Jeffery Thompson (2015), a musician and leading researcher in this field of study, has a Music for Brainwaves CD (and it's a station on Pandora). I recommend using Thompson's music for training or practicing breathing and relaxation exercises. Thompson's CD and other 180-beats-per-minute music can be purchased online and used to train the brain for deep sleep, improved mental focus, and enhanced athletic performance.

Cued Relaxation

Relaxation techniques like the ones just learned (i.e., belly breathing, square breathing, PMR) are often practiced in the comfort of one's own home with plenty of time to relax. Sometimes, athletes can relax off the field but struggle to relax quickly when they are tense before or during a competition. Athletes and coaches need techniques they can use on the spot. In this section, we discuss how to use cued relaxation to trigger the relaxation response in competition.

Cued relaxation is an abbreviated form of the relaxation strategies in this chapter. Although belly breathing and PMR are valuable relaxation tools, they initially take 10 to 20 minutes of practice and most sports don't allow 10 minutes to relax. Cued relaxation takes these lengthier relaxation techniques and shortens them to work instantaneously, generally within 3 to 5 seconds.

Practicing Cued Relaxation

Cued relaxation allows individuals to develop a strong association between a word and the feeling of being totally relaxed. To practice cued relaxation, first deeply relax by using a relaxation technique of your choice (i.e., belly breathing, PMR, etc.). Then, on a scale of 1 to 10, 1 being totally relaxed and 10 being very tense, relax to a level that matches a score of 3 or below.

Next, think of a relaxation cue word (e.g., peaceful, light, calm) that describes this state of deep relaxation. While deeply breathing, say this cue word silently on every exhale for at least 3 minutes or 15 breaths. This word is a self-directed cue meant to strengthen the association between your word and total relaxation in your mind and body. It is a cue to help the body remember this relaxed state. With practice, cued relaxation is meant to work within 3 to 5 seconds.

After an athlete gains experience practicing cued relaxation at home, have them try to implement this skill during training or practice. For example, at the end of a practice session finish the cool down with one to five deep belly breaths. Then, have the athlete repeat their cue word silently to themselves with each exhalation for at least 3 minutes or 15 breaths.

To further master cued relaxation, identify three times in practice when you or the athletes you coach are overaroused and need to relax. During these times, take one to three deep belly breaths (or relaxation technique of your choice) and repeat your cued relaxation word silently on every exhale. Assess your arousal level on the arousal continuum scale from Chapter 4 on page 65 to ensure that you are in a zone where your arousal is low enough that tension is released but not too low where it interferes with performance. In other words, arousal is lowered, yet is high enough for engagement. Within a few days, you should see an improved ability to lower arousal level when necessary. Within a few weeks, your ability to relax on command should be at an optimal level and ready to use it in competition.

In competition, Phil Jackson, coach of 11 NBA championships, used cued relaxation in basketball games by taking the first few seconds of a time-out to have his athletes relax, re-center, and refocus on performing at their optimal zone of functioning (Jackson & Delehanty, 2006). Cued relaxation can be used as a powerful tool in competition as well as pre-performance routines, such as before free throws in basketball, putting in golf, sending a climbing route, or kicking a field goal in football. Endurance sports that typically do not have breaks in competition, like swimming, running, and soccer, can also benefit from cued relaxation to release any muscle tightness during the fire of competition or to let go when dwelling on a mistake. It's important to point out that using cued relaxation in competition is most beneficial when it's been practiced and mastered in training.

To sum up the importance of becoming skilled at relaxation, I think Tim Gallwey (2010), author of *The Inner Game of Tennis*, does it best,

> *The player of the inner game comes to value the art of relaxed concentration above all other skills; he discovers a true basis for self-confidence; and he learns that the secret to winning any game lies in not trying too hard. He aims at the kind of spontaneous performance which occurs only when the mind is calm and seems at one with the body, which finds its own surprising ways to surpass its own limits again and again.*

Relaxation is a powerful tool to help this golfer regulate his arousal and optimize putting performance

Energize to Revitalize

Energization is the opposite of relaxation. *Energization* skills help athletes to speed up heart rate and respiratory rate to improve blood flow to the brain and body, thus getting the most out of their practice and performance. By using energization techniques athletes are better able to draw on their energy reserves when drive is low, such as needing enthusiasm in practice, lacking motivation with a necessary maximum effort, losing focus late in the game, playing against a significantly weaker opponent, or getting bummed after a mistake. It can be a huge confidence builder for athletes to know how to drum up their energy reserves when it matters most. However, various energizing strategies used by coaches to *psych up* athletes are used inappropriately (Weinberg & Gould, 2014). Strategies such as motivational speeches or pep talks can overarouse athletes. If arousal is to be raised, then be mindful that it is done with a goal of reaching an optimal state of arousal. Three energization techniques discussed in this section are: *power breathing, ray of sunshine imagery, and music.*

Power Breathing

Power breathing is meant to increase respiratory rate and stimulate the sympathetic nervous system. This technique requires quick, shallow breathing where athletes use less of their diaphragm (as in relaxation techniques) and more of their lungs which is effective in elevating arousal levels. Increasing respiratory rate also increases carbon dioxide removal from circulation, thus, increasing the amount of time that an athlete can sprint or give a maximal effort before accumulating carbon dioxide registers in the medulla oblongata and stimulates the nociceptors, a sensory receptor that signals pain to the brain warning us to stop (McArdle, Katch, & Katch, 2010). Athletes can use power breathing to give a maximal effort, block out a distracting crowd, or boost motivation during mundane drills at practice. For example, a discus thrower might use short, quick breaths before an all-out effort, a soccer player might breathe fast and forceful to beat an opponent to the ball, or a climber uses power breathing during a crux move to block out distracting thoughts as well as enhance physiological performance factors.

Like relaxation, energization is a mental training tool that needs to be practiced and personalized so that it can be effective during the heat of competition. Practice with the following power-breathing exercise to boost mental and physical performance.

Mental Exercise: Power-Breathing Script

As with relaxation, find a quiet place to practice. Sustain proper body alignment throughout your practice. Place both hands over your rib cage with your fingers pointing toward the midline over your sternum. Move your hands so that of both your middle fingers are touching each other. With quick breaths, begin to inhale rapidly through your nose so that your middle fingertips slightly move away from each other. With a short exhale, breathe out through your nose allowing the middle fingertips to come back together and touch each other. Continue the quick shallow breathing for a few breaths. Discontinue power breathing if you start to feel light headed. Because the nature of competition is dynamic, the power-breathing technique can be a fast and effective way to gain more energy on command.

Practicing Power Breathing

Before practicing power breathing, assess your arousal level on the scale from Chapter 4. Power breathe for 10 to 30 seconds and reassess your arousal level. Are you in your zone of optimal functioning? Practice power breathing every day so you are able to reach your zone of optimal functioning.

Ray of Sunshine Imagery

Imagery is another way to gain energy. Athletes can use imagery as a technique to gain power, strength, and positivity to promote recovery or optimize performance. Energization imagery is centered on the idea that if one can't change the low energy environment around them, they can still change the environment within. The ability to use imagery to improve performance is one of the most powerful tools in the mental skills toolshed, yet it is seldom used by athletes or taught by coaches. It is possible to harness the power of the mind to self-energize during a tough workout, a gloomy injury, or when distracting thoughts pop up.

The ray of sunshine imagery is an example of how to use the mind as a source that energizes and heals. The ray of sunshine imagery may be a new and unfamiliar mental tool, consequently, outside one's comfort zone. However, this technique is especially effective for athletes recovering from an injury, illness, or competition or preparing for a tough workout.

Mental Exercise: Ray of Sunshine Imagery Script

Begin by getting into a comfortable position. Inhale and exhale naturally. As you become more present in the moment, start to imagine a radiant yellow beam of sunlight entering the top of your head. Notice the tingling sensation that is growing at the top of your head. Bring all your attention to this area. Begin to let the radiant energy and light pour down through your body, moving from the top of your head, down to your neck and shoulders and radiating out through your fingertips. See and feel the vibrant light move through your upper body as it trickles down through your spine, chest, and stomach. The radiant yellow beam of sunlight begins to easily flow down through your pelvis, your legs and into your feet. Simply experience the vibrant energy flowing and pulsating throughout your entire body.

Allow this radiant yellow beam disintegrate all mental and physical challenges. Let it suck away all the waste, impurities, heaviness, and problems that hold you back. As you allow yourself to let go of challenges, feel yourself getting stronger. You notice your body is gaining more power, more strength, and more stamina until your energy level is at your optimal zone of functioning.

From this energized state, create a cue or signal for yourself that will allow you to remember this feeling. To do this, decide on a word that describes what you are feeling in this moment, like *power, sunshine,* or *explosive* or choose a physical cue, such as *rubbing your hands together, clenching and releasing your fists three times* or *jumping up and down.* Deeply feel the sensation of being energized as you perform your cue. Tell yourself that you will return to this energized state whenever you perform this cue. Practice using your cue for 3 minutes or 15 to 20 breaths. To improve your arousal level and gain energy on command, return to this personalized cue and experience the energy you need to perform at your best—on and off the field.

To end this practice, slowly count down from five to one. With each number, become more in touch with what's going on around you. As you reach one, open your eyes and remain confident, energized, and full of strength.

Imagery to Energize

The ray of sunshine imagery allows athletes to imagine receiving energy from an outside source but athletes can also gain energy by imagining a past experience where they felt completely motivated, energetic, and confident. For example, athletes can vividly recreate a competitive experience where they felt strong, experienced excitement, and performed at the top of their game. To gain energy and reach a zone of optimal functioning from imagining a past peak experience, it's important for athletes to use all their senses to see, hear, feel, touch, taste, and smell as well as incorporate ideal moods and emotions (see Chapter 6 for details on imagery). The goal is to focus on recalling a past performance where athletes felt energized, yet poised. Athletes can also imagine something that is energizing to them, such as a sprinter imagining a gazelle quickly running over the plains or a swimmer moving through water like a dolphin. If athletes practice imagining ideal zones of optimal functioning, then they develop a powerful ability to energize themselves to an ideal level of arousal and reach their full potential.

Practicing Energizing Imagery

Mastering energizing imagery typically takes a minimum of 2 to 3 weeks of consistent practice. Because it's hard to recover from a bad start, a good time to practice energization imagery is once you get out of bed in the morning or before a training session. With practice, you'll be able to use imagery to gain energy, focus, and be centered in the present moment.

Music to Energize

Previously discussed was how music can be used to relax, yet music can also be used to energize. The beat, tempo, and rhythm of catchy, upbeat music has energizing effects. Marcus Pollard, NFL tight end, spoke about music and mental training to improve sports performance at a sport psychology conference I attended a few years ago (Eckstein, Pollard, & McGill, 2012). To get physically and mentally ready for the game, Marcus said he used the same music playlist for all 13 years of his NFL career. Each song had a particular rhythm, beat, and lyrics that he used to enhance his energy level, to feel explosive before competition, and to get him into the right head space before a grueling game.

The mechanisms by which music helps us to gain energy isn't exactly clear, yet what is known is that music can alter psychological and physical elements. Music has the ability to cause the brain to release dopamine. Among other things, this neurotransmitter improves the rate of decision making and decreases rating of perceived exertion (McConnell, 2009). Self-selected, energizing music also increases heart rate and respiratory rate to prime us for improved work output and better athletic performance as well as enhancing positive mood states which diverts our attention away from fatigue and discomfort (Karageorghis & Priest, 2012; Karageorghis & Terry, 1997). Examples of ways that music can help us draw on our inner energy includes: a gymnast playing fast-paced tunes to feel powerful during a floor routine, a cross country skier replaying an upbeat song in his or her head to maintain speed and power on a tough climb, or a mountain biker listening to high energy music during a ride.

Also, a note of caution regarding how one chooses to consume music. Using music to get motivated before or during every practice can be desensitizing. Just like caffeine, music loses it boosting effects if it's used too much (Greenfield, 2014). Music is recommend for hard workouts, such as interval or superset workouts or when you feel low and need extra motivation to elevate arousal before practice. Also consider reserving a special pre-performance playlist for use only before games or competitions (like NFL linebacker Marcus Pollard).

Cued Energization

Like cued relaxation, cued energization is an abbreviated form of energization exercises. *Cued energization* pairs a cue word with feelings of being energized. Because of the time limited nature of competition, cued energization is a technique meant to be used when an athlete needs a booster shot of energy on the fly.

Practicing Cued Energization

Sport psychology coaches Damon Burton and Thomas Raedeke (2008) recommend cued energization be mastered in three basic steps. The three steps to learn and use cued energization are the same steps used in cued relaxation. First, the athlete goes through an energization skill that works well for him or her. Second, the athlete selects a cue word that is associated with feeling highly energized (e.g., strong, powerful, explosive, unstoppable) and repeats the cue word after each breath for 15 to 20 breaths. Third, the athlete uses cued energization to gain energy in 3 to 5 seconds by taking six power breaths and repeating the cue word silently to themselves after each breath. With practice, athletes can gain the kind of energy needed to play to their potential within a few seconds.

To sum, athletes, coaches, public speakers, or professionals who perform at a high level recognize the importance of finding that centered place inside of themselves to perform optimally. People may notice their mounting stress or dwindling energy but few know how to channel their energy to stay in their optimal zone of functioning. This chapter provides you with practical and palatable ways to properly manage your energy to live and perform to your unique potential.

The next chapter illuminates another component of a champion mindset—imagery. Chapter 6 explains what imagery is and discusses the key steps in helping athletes learn how to use imagery to improve performance.

Summary

- Top performers need to have the ability to relax and energize so they can quickly adjust their arousal levels and perform their best.
- Relaxation sparks mental and physical responses which counter the detrimental effects of stress. Relaxation improves breathing, calms the mind, decreases excessive stress hormones and reduces unnecessary muscle tension.
- To help athletes completely relax, four strategies, scripts, and practice techniques were introduced in this chapter: belly breathing, square breathing, progressive muscle relaxation, and music.
- Cued relaxation is a learned skill that pairs a self-instructed cue word with feelings of deep relaxation to promote optimal relaxation and performance in 3 to 5 seconds.
- Energization helps athletes draw on their energy reserves when energy is low or when focus has been lost. Energization techniques can help athletes elevate their arousal level to an optimal level and boost confidence.
- Three energization techniques to improve performance were presented in this chapter: power breathing, ray of sunshine imagery, and music.
- Cued energization pairs a cue word with feelings of high energy to foster the optimal arousal level needed to perform one's best. Cued energization is taught after energization exercises have been learned and practiced.

- Relaxation and energization skills are practical tools for athletes to manage their arousal levels and enhance performance. Developing your ability to relax your body and calm your mind is an essential element in performance and health because it allows you to control and channel your arousal, intensity, and tension appropriately.

References

Burton, D., & Raedeke, T. D. (2008). Relaxation and energization. In *Sport Psychology for Coaches* (pp. 83–100). Champaign, IL: Human Kinetics.

Bood, R. J., Nijssen, M., Van Der Kamp, J., & Roerdink, M. (2013). The power of auditory-motor synchronization in sports: Enhancing running performance by coupling cadence with the right beats. *PloS one, 8*(8), e70758.

Davidson, R. J., & Begley, S. (2013). *The emotional life of your brain: How its unique patterns affect the way you think, and live—and how you can change them*. First Plume Printing.

Davidson, R. J., Kabat-Zinn, J., Schumacher, J., Rosenkranz, M., Muller, D., Santorelli, S. F., Urbanowski, F., Harrington, A., Bonus, K., & Sheridan, J. F. (2003). Alterations in brain and immune function produced by mindfulness meditation. *Psychosomatic medicine, 65*(4), 564–570.

Draganski, B., Gaser, C., Busch, V., Schuierer, G., Bogdahn, U., & May, A. (2004). Neuroplasticity: Changes in grey matter induced by training. *Nature, 427*(6972), 311–312.

Eckstein, D., Pollard, M., & McGill, T. (2012) *Invited performance psychology interview*. Atlanta, GA: Association of Applied Sports Psychology Conference.

Graham, L., & Hanson, R. (2013). *Bouncing back: Rewiring your brain for maximum resilience and well-being*. New World Library.

Greenfield, B. (2014). *Beyond training: Mastering endurance, health and life*. Victory Belt Publishing.

Gallwey, W. T. (2010). *The inner game of tennis: The classic guide to the mental side of peak performance*. Random House.

Jackson, P., & Delehanty, H. (2006). *Sacred hoops: Spiritual lessons of a hardwood warrior*. Hyperion.

Jacobson, E. (1938). *Progressive relaxation*. Chicago: University of Chicago Press.

Karageorghis, C. I., & Priest, D. L. (2012). Music in the exercise domain: a review and synthesis (Part II). *International review of sport and exercise psychology, 5*(1), 67–84.

Karageorghis, C. I., & Terry, P. C. (1997). The psychophysical effects of music in sport and exercise: A review. *Journal of Sport Behavior, 20*, 54–68.

Martens, R. (1987). *Coaches guide to sport psychology.* Champaign, IL: Human Kinetics.

McArdle, W. D., Katch, F. I., & Katch, V. L. (2010). *Exercise physiology: nutrition, energy, and human performance.* Lippincott Williams & Wilkins.

McConnell, A. K. (2009). Respiratory muscle training as an ergogenic aid. *Journal of Exercise Science & Fitness, 7*(2), S18–S27.

Miyachi, T., Kurita, D., Iga, S., & Furuhata, T. (2014). An Relationship between Stress-less and Comfortable Acoustic Information, and Asymmetry Changes in Hemoglobin Concentrations. *Procedia Computer Science, 35,* 1278–1283.

Mumford, G. (2015). *The mindful athlete: Secrets to pure performance.* Berkley, CA: Parallax Press.

Schneider, S., Askew, C. D., Abel, T., & Strüder, H. K. (2010). Exercise, music, and the brain: Is there a central pattern generator?. *Journal of sports sciences, 28*(12), 1337–1343.

Schwartz, M. S., & Andrasik, F. (Eds.). (2015). *Biofeedback: A practitioner's guide.* Guilford Publications.

Strack B.W., & Gervirtz, R. (2011). Getting to the Heart of the Matter: Heart Rate Variability Biofeedback for Enhanced Performance. In B. W. Strack, M. K. Linden, V. S. Wilson (eds.), *Biofeedback & Neurofeedback Applications in Sport Psychology. Association for Applied Psychophysiology and Biofeedback Conference* (pp. 145–74). Retrieved Nov 28, 2016 https://resourcenter.net/images/AAPB/Bookstore/AAPB_Sport_Psych_DRAFT.pdf

Thompson, J. D. (2015). *U.S. Patent No. 8,932,218.* Washington, DC: U.S. Patent and Trademark Office.

Winter, B. (1981). *Relax & Win: Championship Performance in Whatever You Do.* As Barnes.

Yasuma, F., & Hayano, J. I. (2004). Respiratory sinus arrhythmia: why does the heartbeat synchronize with respiratory rhythm?. *Chest Journal, 125*(2), 683–690.

CHAPTER 6

Imagery: Visualize to Actualize

"A big part of my training has been visualization—I try to put myself in race situations. It starts when I lace up my skates and I go through every possible scenario in the race, the crowd, even the people watching from home. I see the race from various angles, starting first or second, leading and sometimes coming from the back of the pack."
—Isabelle Charest, Olympic Short-Track Speed Skater

Many top performers value the power of imagery. For example, on June 3, 2017 Alex Honnold did the unthinkable. Honnold became the first rock climber to free solo (climbing without the use of ropes or safety gear) Yosemite's 3,000-foot El Capitan wall via Freerider (VI, 5.13a) in 3 hours, 56 minutes. To help him prepare for possibly the greatest feat of pure rock climbing in the history of the sport, Honnold used imagery to help him train. Not only did he physically train for the daring climb for more than a year, he also spent a great deal of time using imagery to remember and rehearse the moves on the route Freerider. This free solo accomplishment sets an unthinkable benchmark in the climbing world as well as the sports world—comparable to when Roger Bannister broke the four-minute mile in 1954.

Whether you are an elite athlete or recreational athlete, I bet you use imagery more often than you think. For example, take a moment to think back to one of your best competitions or best life experiences. Picture where it took place. Experience how you felt in that moment. Can you recall what smells were in the air? What kinds of thoughts did you experience? Can you see your competitors, fans, and the venue in bright, clear images? Recreating our past successes and making them as real as possible is one example of how we use mental imagery.

Imagery is also a mental training tool that athletes, successful entre-preneurs, highly skilled surgeons, and accomplished musicians use to strengthen their ability to achieve excellence. Because imagery is mul-tifaceted and used in multiple domains, the purpose of this chapter is to: define imagery, discuss evidence related to the mechanisms by which imagery acts to improve performance, and learn to use imagery effectively as a tool to optimize training and performance.

What Is Imagery?

Imagery is using the mind's eye to create or recreate an experience (Vealey & Greenleaf, 2001). Visualization, mental rehearsal, symbolic rehearsal, mental practice, or covert practice are other concepts that have been used to describe imagery. All these concepts explain the essence of imagery, which is the process of using all of your senses to feel, smell, hear, taste, pic-ture, and fully experience an image or to dream something. For example, dancers can combine past memories of dance movements and sequences they have done in previous attempts and create an image in their mind and feelings in their body of how they want the routine to flow.

Imagery can also be thought of as an active form of meditation. By experiencing actions through your mind's eye, you can tap into your inner source of calmness, become centered, and choose images that influence you to respond positively in an uncertain situation. This is because what you see in your mind's eye can strongly influence emotions, energy, and achievements. As Napoleon Hill, the early 20th-century author is famous for saying, "Whatever the mind of man can conceive and believe, it can achieve."

To illustrate how imagery can influence the senses, I invite you to imagine an orange slice by using the following example.

Mental Exercise: Orange Slice

Close your eyes for a moment and imagine yourself relaxed in the kitchen. In your mind's eye, begin to notice the color of the counter-top. Imagine the time of day and how the light hits the countertops. Hear the hum of the refrigerator. Notice the plump, juicy orange lying on a cutting board. Pick it up and feel its weight. Feel the texture of the dimpled, glossy skin. With a sharp knife, carefully cut a large slice. Notice the fragrant juices as they trickle onto the countertop. Lift the orange slice to your mouth. Smell it's sweet, fresh scent. Place the orange slice into your mouth and bite down. Is your mouth watering?

The orange slice exercise causes most people to salivate. We salivate not because imagery is magic. Rather, imagery is an incredibly powerful tool which enables the mind's eye to influence emotions, perceptions, and energy. Many individuals do not feel as though they have control over how their mind and body operates and leave it up to the expert doctors to heal them or save them from suffering. Granted, if I have a broken leg then I definitely want a trained doctor to help me. But it is also important to understand that we have much more control than we think. It's simply learning to understand, navigate, and influence the mind and body in order to experience the power of achieving the things that matter most.

How Imagery Works

Like all mental training, imagery is a skill. When practiced regularly, imagery enables an individual to perform to their potential or beyond. Imagery acts like a dress rehearsal and puts one into the right frame of mind. By practicing for the task ahead (e.g., having the power for a max bench press, learning a new acrobatic skill, letting go of pressure), it is possible to have a sense of what to expect, thus, the dress rehearsal in the mind makes everything seem more familiar and easier. On the flip side, images that are viewed as negative can create a state of over- or under-arousal and hinder performance but when positive images are perceived there are improved attitude, attention, and optimal arousal levels.

From a physiological perspective, imagery works because the central nervous system does not differentiate between real and imaginary. The brain sees all images as if they are real (i.e., remember imagining the orange slice and salivating). For example, an athlete may feel uneasy the night before a big competition because he or she fears performing poorly.

The competition may feel threatening because the athlete fears they will fail in front of others. On the other hand, take the real life situation of walking in the woods and being suddenly startled by a grizzly bear with her cubs. In this situation one is also likely to feel very nervous. Both events, the competition and the bear encounter, can cause great anxiety. However, feeling incredibly nervous before a competition is a perception of the situation (i.e., an imagined event) and encountering the mama grizzly bear is a real threat. Yet, the brain doesn't differentiate between real and imaginary. The brain simply responds to the perceived or real threat and releases the necessary physiological changes (i.e., increased heart rate, increased attention) to avoid the threat, fight the threat, or just survive.

Imagery uses the mind's eye in conjunction with the senses to create an experience that feels real. When using imagery the brain is creating a mental blueprint of potential movements and actions. Imagery can help an athlete perform at their best because they are ingraining and strengthening neural pathways associated with the imagined events. Mental blueprints can include recreating a successful past performance to gain confidence or imagining the sequencing and timing of a sport skill. For example, imagining a physical movement or sports skill (such as a 720 rotation in skateboarding) helps an athlete to better understand where the body needs to be relative to the space surrounding them, this allows an athlete to more seamlessly perform the skill in real-time. When we imagine something, we are asking the mind to trace the blueprint of a motor program, past experience, or future event so that the neural pathway becomes automatic, which increases the chances of a successful outcome.

Imagery can also be used to learn how to automatically respond to certain situations. For instance, a soccer player who's susceptible to being emotionally reactive in games may clench his fist and subsequently relax his fingers while imaging an opponent heatedly talking in his face and trying to get under his skin. Another example is the volleyball player who struggles with overarousal and chokes during games. The volleyball player allows the excitement, nervousness, and worry of the game to surface during her imagery practice. Then, she imagines herself being at her optimal zone of arousal by using relaxation tools before and during the game to play confidently. As a result, images in our mind's eye influence what we believe, how we act, and what we achieve.

Imagery involves using all the senses to create or recreate an experience in the mind and provides athletes a mental tool to achieve higher levels of performance

Another example of how imagery works to foster performance is golfing legend Jack Nicklaus. In his book, *Golf My Way*, he says that an effective golf shot is 10 percent swing, 40 percent set up, and 50 percent the mental picture of an optimal swing. Nicklaus says:

> *I never hit a shot, even in practice, without having a very sharp, in-focus picture of it in my head. It's like a color movie. First I "see" the ball where I want it to finish, nice and white and sitting up high on the bright green grass. Then the scene quickly changes and I "see" the ball going there: its path, trajectory, and shape, even its behavior on landing. Then there is a sort of fade-out, and the next scene shows me making the kind of swing that will turn the images into reality (Nicklaus, 1974, p.79).*

Imagery is sometimes abstract. Most athletes and coaches I know like more concrete ways of demonstrating mental training. To help understand how imagery works and make it more tangible, I use either the orange imagery exercise or the bolt on a string activity (see the following mental exercise). When athletes and coaches are better equipped to understand how imagery works, then they are more likely to practice and benefit from imagery.

Mental Exercise: Bolt on a String Imagery

Activity: Use a flat metal washer and a 10- to 15-inch piece of string. A paper clip and dental floss can substitute for the washer and string. Tie the string to a washer. Then, steady the elbows on a table or flat surface. Next, hold the string between the index finger and thumb of both hands about 6 to 10 inches away from the face. Hold the hands as steady as possible and imagine the washer move back and forth with the eyes, swinging side to side like a pendulum of a clock, without using the fingers to swing the washer. Start with imagining small movements and progress to seeing the bolt making bigger pendulum swings. Then, try to slow the swinging. Begin to imagine the bolt moving in a clockwise circle (through the mind's eye). Now try moving the bolt counter-clockwise.

Discussion: In most instances athletes report movement in their bolts without purposefully moving it with their fingers. Inform the athletes that there are subtle impulses sent from the brain to the hands as a result of the mental imagery, and these muscle impulses are responsible for the movement in the bolt. When using imagery, your brain is creating a mental blueprint of your movements. Therefore, you are ingraining and strengthening the blueprint of the movement so that it becomes part of the neural and muscle memory network. This practice is not at the same amplitude or intensity as if actually performing the activity but the timing and rhythm is similar. Take a moment to think about how this concept and how it can be applied to a specific sport or activity.

Four Main Theories of Imagery

In an effort to introduce more detailed information, the four following imagery theories are introduced: *psychoneuromuscular theory, symbolic learning theory, bioinformational theory,* and the *triple code model*.

The *psychoneuromuscular theory* (Carpenter, 1984) theorizes that imagery fosters improved performance because vividly imagined events innervate the muscles in a similar way as physically practicing a movement which, in turn, strengthen neural pathways. This is the explanation used in the previous mental exercise, the bolt on a string. It is theorized that imagery acts as a way to program the muscles for specific movements because the imagined events are innervating the same muscles as the actual movement. During imagery, the muscle innervation is not to the same amplitude or intensity as if the actual movement were occurring but the firing rate and rhythm is similar.

The *symbolic learning theory*, introduced by Sackett (1934), states that imagery functions as a coding system (i.e., mental blueprint) to help people understand and acquire movement patterns and rehearse cognitive components. An athlete learns a skill by familiarizing themselves with what needs to be done to execute the skill successfully. This suggests every motion has a blueprint, or coding system, used to execute a movement. Subconsciously this blueprint, or code, is called upon when a specific task is executed (such as shooting a free throw, making a turn on skis, or bunny-hopping over a log). When an athlete practices imagery of a specific skill, they are essentially asking the mind to initiate a movement (i.e., find the blueprint) and engage in that movement (i.e., execute the code). Imagery is tracing the blueprint of the motor program, which helps to develop a code for that movement.

The following scenario is another example of how the symbolic learning theory can be applied to American Football. A football quarterback has to execute multiple dynamic movements in any given play series. Since I'm a Green Bay Packers fan, I'll use quarterback Aaron Rodgers as an example. When Rodgers prepares for a game he likely uses imagery. He creates a strategy, develops a pattern in his head, and makes an action plan. By using imagery to develop a plan, he's more likely to implement that plan because the details have already been coded into a mental blueprint, which allows him to execute successful plays. The more he practices the imagery the more lifelike the images and the more likely he is to correctly execute the plan during the actual game.

These first two theories (psychoneuromuscular theory and symbolic learning theory) are complimentary to each other. The next two theories *bioinformational theory* and *triple code model* are also complimentary.

The *bioinformational theory* (Lang, 1979) states an image has two main components: stimulus propositions and response propositions.

- *Stimulus propositions* are the characteristics of the image. It's the images color, shape, and texture and what it does.
- *Response propositions* describe the athlete's response to the image, which produces a muscular and psychological response.

For example, a response proposition is like a big-mountain skier imagining herself dropping into a steep, tight couloir and responds with her heart pounding and simultaneously her face smiling. She responds with both fear of falling and excitement for the adventure. This means bioinformational theory is beyond the imagined picture. It is the emotion and the engagement of that emotion, action, or skill. In order for imagery to occur, there needs to be both the stimulus (i.e., what you encounter) and the response (i.e., what will you do).

Ahsen's (1984) *triple code model* goes a step further and places meaning into imagery, which is known as ISM. The first part is the *image* (I). The image is a clearly and fully described scene (i.e., outside world). The second part is *somatic response* (S). The somatic response refers to the psychophysiological changes occurring, such as experiencing positive thoughts or sweaty palms (i.e., inside world). The third part of the triple code model is *meaning* (M).

Unlike the other theories, the triple code model suggests that every image needs to have a sense of personal meaning, significance, or importance. Because people place different meanings and values on different things, the same set of imagery instructions given to all imagers will not create the same imagery experience for any two people. The triple code model encourages us to engage the imager in a much deeper manner and seek to discover the meanings behind the images of each individual. When there is a better understanding of the meaning and emotional reactions to an event, it is possible to account for those emotions within an imagery session. This kind of preparedness breeds confidence and consistency, thus, helping an athlete to perform with confidence and consistency.

All of these theories have supporting evidence but there isn't agreement among experts as to which is the most likely. It is probable that imagery increases performance via multiple mechanisms. Future research using technological advances may help us to better understand how and why imagery works.

Imagery fosters improved performance and goal achievement through multiple mechanisms, such as placing meaning or significance on an image to reach an aspiration

Using Imagery to Improve Performance

In addition to the previously described theories, there are more than 200 studies that support imagery as an effective tool for optimizing performance in a wide variety of sports (Martin, Moritz & Hall, 1999). For example, highly skilled athletes use imagery more regularly than less accomplished athletes (Cumming & Hall, 2002). In a survey studying United States and Canadian Olympic athletes, about 90 percent reported using imagery (Murphy, Jowdy & Durtschi, 1990; Orlick & Parrington, 1988). These athletes, on average, practiced imagery 4 days a week for 10 to 15 minutes at a time. Some athletes spent 2 to 3 hours engaging in imagery to prepare for their event prior to the Olympic Games.

Although there is plenty of evidence to support the use of imagery as a means to improve performance (for reviews, see Cumming & Ramsey, 2009; Murphy, Nordin, & Cumming, 2008; Parnabas, Parnabas, & Parnabas, 2015), research also shows that imagery works best as a supplement to physical practice, not as a replacement for training (Hird, Landers, Thomas, & Horan, 1991; Kumar, 2015). In other words, imagery alone is less effective than physical practice. However, it is more effective to use imagery in addition to physical practice than physical practice alone. Best practices, then, are the combination of physical training and mental imagery.

Imagery is also a flexible tool that can be used and practiced almost anywhere, any time, and for a number of uses on and off the field. For example, coaches and athletes can take a couple of minutes before practice to imagine how they want practice to flow. One summer I coached three professional sport climbers on mental skill enhancement during a 3-month boot camp training program as a way to improve their climbing ability. Before a climbing session, one of the athletes, we'll call him Drake, approached me about not sleeping well the night before due to an argument he had earlier. After some further inquiry about how Drake was doing, I took him through a 5-minute imagery session that included: visualizing the argument, letting go of the argument, checking in with where he was at in this moment—physically, mentally, and emotionally, then had him imagine releasing all the things that he was holding on to and visualizing how he wanted to transition from the present moment into the climbing training session. We ended the imagery session with creating a word or image that captured the essence of how he wanted to train that day.

In the middle of that same training session, there was a squabble between the climbing coach and one of the other climbers about team dynamics. The climbing coach sat everyone down and had a meeting. Part of the discussion was on attitude and mindset. Drake, the climber who went through the guided imagery earlier that day, spoke up. He said,

I had a crappy night. I woke up in a bad mood and I didn't want to train today. I told Chris and she took me through this imagery and I imagined todays training flowing like a river. To my surprise, I'm having a great training day. I think that the guided imagery Chris took me through is directly related to me having a good vs bad training day.

One of the powers of imagery is that within a few minutes athletes can change their mindset to help them train or perform at a high level. Coaches and athletes can also use imagery to maintain sports skills, such as when practice is cancelled due to unplayable weather conditions, on days of physical rest, or when an athlete is ill or injured.

Scientifically, there is even evidence to support the role of imagery as a means to promote healing. In the seminal research of Jon Kabat-Zinn and colleagues (1998), investigators had participants with moderate to severe psoriasis use mindfulness meditation and guided imagery in combination with phototherapy (light box) to reduce the effects of the disease. Those who listened to the imagery audio recordings during their treatment in the light box experienced clearing of the skin at a rate almost four times faster than those who received the light treatment alone. Anecdotally, I had a 47-year-old climbing athlete who imagined a healing bright light seep into the dark, broken areas of her foot and the doctors were amazed how fast she healed.

Imagery can be used for a variety of other uses as well, including: improved motivation, technique, skill development, evaluating one's performance, and pain reduction. Following are some detailed examples of how imagery can improve performance and personal excellence:

- *Motivation*: Athletes can use motivating self-talk and images such as, "I see myself as stronger, fitter, and more confident than ever before." Other motivational uses of imagery include visualizing oneself as persistent and flexible (e.g., "When unexpected barriers arise, I easily recognize them, effortlessly hurdle over them, and simply stay with the task at hand"), experiencing future goal attainment (e.g., "I see myself finishing the marathon") or seeing successful past performances (e.g., "I'm capable of reaching higher than my previous best").
- *Technique*: When learning a new skill, athletes can slow down images to better understand and analyze technique. Skilled athletes can imagine reducing complex movements into simple skills in order to refine and master a challenging task. After learning the new skill it is important to imagine technique and skills in real time. Also, overly fatigued athletes can mentally practice with good form rather than physically practice with poor form; this can help an athlete avoid ingraining bad habits, overtraining syndrome, or sustaining a fatigue-related injury.
- *Coping*: Imagining different game situations and planning strategies in advance is an effective imagery tool. For example, Michael Phelps was on the starting blocks for the 200-meter

race at 2008 Olympics Games. The starting gun went off and
he exploded into the water. Suddenly, his goggles began to
fill with water. Rather than freak out, he had imagined this
situation and had a plan...count strokes. Phelps counted his
strokes for each length of the pool. The last length he finished
strong, touched the wall, took off his goggles and looked
at scoreboard. He set a world record, despite adversity, and
won an Olympic gold medal! In addition, after a less than
ideal performance athletes can imagine replaying a more
appropriate response to an unexpected challenge and regain
confidence.

- *Manage Energy*: Imagining a calm scene is an effective way to
  relax and manage energy when an athlete is overaroused or
  seems to care *too much*. Equally effective is visualizing energizing images to get athletes psyched to meet an upcoming
  challenge (see Chapter 5).

- *Evaluate Performance*: After a practice session or competition
  an athlete can replay his or her performance to reinforce what
  went well and rehearse a targeted area of improvement. The
  athlete can also rehearse a specific strategy of improvement
  to implement in the future.

- *Depression*: Athletes can imagine all the feelings of sadness
  (or performance blues) attached to a red helium balloon that
  they are tightly holding on to by a string. Next, they can then
  imagine gently letting go of the red balloon and watch it float
  off into a clear, blue sky. As the balloon is set free, they also
  release what is holding them down. The red balloon is also a
  popular technique I teach to athletes who experience performance anxiety and they incorporate releasing the balloon as
  part of their pre-performance routine.

- *Pain*: Athletes can see pain washed away by a calm, cooling
  river flowing through their entire body. Individuals can also
  imagine grabbing a TV remote control and slowly turning
  down the pain volume until it is barely audible and finally
  disappears.

- *Tension*: Athletes can imagine a tight, twisted rope slowly unraveling and becoming more and more loose. Another helpful visual is imagining wax softening and melting as it releases a tight muscle.

Imagery is not limited to the uses discussed in this book. For example, imagery can be used for improving concentration, gaining confidence before a big game, and solving problems. There is even research on the uses of guided imagery to help cancer patients relieve pain (King, 2010). As the research on imagery grows, we are finding fascinating uses of this powerful tool. Imagery has the potential to improve health, happiness, and achieve higher levels of performance. The possibilities are endless and exciting! The next section discusses how to apply and maximize the benefits of using imagery.

Applying Imagery Theories

Mark Tewksbury the Olympic backstroke swimmer describes imagery as a skill: "*The ability to visualize doesn't happen overnight. It can take years to perfect, but by persevering you can eventually see the desired outcome clearly and absolutely in your mind.*" Like all mental skills, imagery is acquired through practice. Some people are good at it right off the bat while others may not even be able to get an image in their mind. I'm the latter, it took me awhile to learn how to use imagery effectively and that's why I'm excited to share the basic elements of how to improve your ability to use imagery.

The key ingredient to using imagery effectively is you. Everyone has unique thoughts, feelings, and images that determine their own reality. This reality is also influenced through an individual's unique set of beliefs, values, and viewpoints. Therefore, it is important that an imagery script is tailored on an individual level. Whether someone is a novice or an elite athlete, all athletes can benefit from using a personalized imagery script. Discussed in this section are the elements of a good imagery script and the tools needed to create an effective personalized script. The hallmarks of an effective imagery script are what I call the *Seven Heavens*.

Seven Heavens: Hallmarks of Effective Imagery

1. Energy Management
2. Multisensory
3. Vividness
4. Controllability
5. Timing
6. Perspective
7. Practice

Energy Management

When first learning to use imagery, practice is most effective when the mind is calm and the body is relaxed. Therefore, it is important to find a quiet spot to relax and avoid being disturbed. Before beginning each athlete should ask, "Where will I practice? My preferred quiet setting is _____."

When first practicing imagery, find a quiet spot to calm the mind and relax the body. (PC: Jamye Chrisman)

As an athlete becomes more skilled in imagery, the next step is to activate the individual zone of functioning (see Chapter 4) while practicing imagined events or skills. When imagery matches one's ideal level of arousal, it activates the appropriate physiological responses needed to execute a skill or prepare for a best attempt (MacIntyre et al., 2013). For example, if imagery is being used to improve a motor skill, like a back tuck on a balance beam, it is necessary that during the imagery session the gymnast matches her energy level to the task requirement (i.e., the back tuck). In other words, the gymnast either calms down or gets psyched up to get within her zone of optimal functioning and properly execute the back tuck in her mind.

Once comfortable with practicing imagery in a quiet, relaxing environment, an athlete can begin to practice imagery in more distracting environments (e.g., in the locker room, at the bus stop). The distractions will be challenging at first, but by deepening the presence within and merging the inner world with the outer world, it is possible to maintain a quiet mind, relaxed body, and clear images. These distracting environments can act as a simulation for competition or an all-out effort, such as if an athlete loses concentration when the crowd cheers or when self-sabotaging thoughts enter the mind.

Regardless of athletic capability, imagery benefits all levels of performers. The following mental exercise below is a great example of how to transition from using the breathing and progressive muscle relaxation exercises from Chapter 5 and introducing imagery in a relaxed, quiet environment.

Mental Exercise: Bedroom Imagery Script

Activity: This is a different spin on the relaxation and progressive muscle relaxation trainings previously introduced, this is an imagery exercise. The first step to successful imagery practice is mastering how to relax. Previously, you practiced breathing as well as tensing and relaxing muscles–becoming fully aware of the difference between tight and loose muscles. Now we are adding another layer to relaxation practice and introducing the new mental skill of imagery. Remember while practicing relaxation, try to just let things happen. Don't make your body relax, allow it to relax.

Lie on your back. As you lay comfortably, close your eyes. Remember to gently adjust your position to make sure you stay comfortable.

As we go through the imagery practice, if your thoughts should wander, it is okay—just bring them back to your breath.

Begin to focus on your breath. Breathe slowly and focus on the inhalation. Fill your lungs completely without forcing anything. Feel the pure, clean air enter your lungs. Enjoy that feeling. Now focus on the exhalation. Feel the used air easily leaving your lungs. Enjoy that feeling. Inhale slowly and deeply—it feels refreshing to breathe so deeply. As you exhale slowly and completely, feel your body begin to sink into the floor just a little more.

On your next inhale, think to yourself *restore*. Inhalation is your body's way of replenishing itself. The fresh, incoming air is nourishing. Take it deeply into your lungs and say to yourself *restore*. As you exhale, think *relax*. Tension lowers and your body effortlessly sinks into the floor. Exhaling so deeply rids your body of the used air, the pressure, the hesitation. Inhale, allow yourself to feel relaxed and refreshed and as you do, say to yourself, *restore*. Exhale, let yourself breathe out fully and as you do so, say to yourself, *relax*. Keep breathing repeating *restore*, *relax*, and sink further into the floor. Enjoy this relaxing feeling. You are calm. You are at peace. You have nowhere to be, but enjoying this very moment.

Now we are going to try some imagery. Imagery is about *your* experience. Don't force yourself to *see* what's described, allow yourself to *experience* images. And *experiment* with using as many senses as you can—sight, sound, taste, hearing, smelling, feeling. Simply do your best to imagine what is being described.

If you can see the images, great. If you can't see it, that's okay too. Imagery is a difficult concept and it takes time to master. Rather than judge yourself, remember you have a choice. Simply do your best and try to remain focused on your experience. Allow yourself to experience this guided image in every way you can. If you experience a lot of detail, pay attention to it. If you experience it in less detail, pay attention to what you do experience.

Let's begin.

Start by imagining a familiar place. I want you to picture your bedroom. First, notice the front door of your bedroom. Slowly walk through the front door and look at your room as a whole. Locate your furniture, the windows, and the door. Feel free to turn around if you'd like to take the whole room in. What's the *temperature* of the room…pleasantly cool or toasty warm? Do you notice any *smells*? Are the smells pungent or pleasant? Take a moment to take in any rich fragrances around you. What *sounds* do you notice? Maybe a fan or a radio you forgot to turn off. Are the sounds loud or soft? Now, turn your attention to your bed, *see* the colors and designs on the bedspread. *Feel* its texture. *Smell* the fragrances.

Now slowly start looking around your room. *See* the pictures on your wall and the clothes in your closet. Does anything that you see impact how you *feel*? If it's a negative feeling can you turn it into a positive? If it's a positive feeling can you savor this feeling? *Feel* the carpet as you walk around your room. If you have to walk over clothes or equipment, does navigating around the mess throw you off balance? Listen closely, can you *hear* your family talking in the background? Maybe you hear the sounds of cars driving by, wind blowing in the trees, or animals chirping outside? Take in a deep breath and let all the things you love about your room seep in. Breathe out and savor this feeling. Take one last moment to note any other things that your senses are picking up on.

That is the completion of the imagery exercise. Please stay relaxed and slowly transition out of the session. Before you open your eyes, think about this imagery exercise. Take a moment to note how many senses and actions you were able to incorporate into your imagery. How clear and vivid were the images? Did the imagery spark any emotions? Now slowly open your eyes and move into a seated position.

I also want to remind you that if you had difficulty doing this exercise, don't worry. Imagery is a skill that takes a lot of practice to develop and perfect. Imagery typically takes 15 minutes of practice per day for 1 to 2 weeks before you start visualizing clear, vivid images. If it was difficult, you may want to explore different special places, such as a favorite training venue, race course, or favorite vacation spot.

Discussion Questions:

1. What did you think?
2. What senses were you able to employ?
3. What emotions related to your images emerged?
4. On a scale of 1 to 10 (1 = low, 10 = high), how would you rate your ability to create clear and vivid images?
5. On a scale of 1 to 10, how would you rate your ability to control the image?
6. How did you see yourself? Were you inside your body as if a camera was on top of your head? Were you outside of your body as if you were watching yourself on TV? Did you see a little of both? If so, do you have a preference for which one you liked?
7. Did the timing work for you...too fast...to slow? How would you change it?

Note: If you are using this imagery script as an introduction to imagery, consider abbreviating this it as it may be too long for the attention span of some athletes.

Multisensory

In the earlier imagery script, the first discussion questions asked you to describe the senses you were able to engage and any related emotions. These questions are important because effective imagery practice is a multisensory approach that requires use of all the senses to create or recreate a lifelike experience.

The key senses used in an imagery session include: vision, kinesthetic, auditory, olfactory, tactile, and taste as well as emotions and moods. The sense of sight is our most dominant sense. Sight is common across most sport domains, thus describing what you see is a critical component to create images that are vivid and realistic.

Kinesthetic sense, or movement of the body, is also a dominant sense. Yet describing how it feels to move through space, water, snow, or sand during an imagery script, is often overlooked. Because athletes are expert feelers (i.e., kinesthetic learners), it is important to remember to high-light how the body moves through space when creating an imagery script. For example, a swimmer streamlining strongly and smoothly through the clear, slippery water.

Smell and taste are other significant senses that are often left out of imagery scripts. Recall at the beginning of this chapter, imagining the slice of orange and your mouth watering. Smelling and tasting seals the deal for images. When we incorporate our sense of smell and taste, like a runner's salty sweat or swimming in chlorinated water, the images we create in our mind's eye really come alive, and help to grease the groove of the mental blueprint. That's because our sense of smell is the fastest way to bring us into the present moment. Our olfactory nerve (smell) zips directly to the ancient structure in our brain, the limbic system. The lim-bic system is our emotional and sensory center. Imagining specific smells

Key senses used in an imagery are: vision, kinesthetic, auditory, olfactory, tactile, and taste as well as emotions and moods

and tastes creates an immediate reaction because this memory doesn't take a detour to other parts of our brain. Imagining smells and tastes associated with our sport can instantly take us to the imagined event.

Lastly, it is important to create meaning into your images. Better understanding the meaning, mood, and emotions behind images sparks excitement, which helps create the necessary physiological changes (e.g., increase focus, heart rate, sweat) to perform optimally. The more meaning and depth attached to the image, the more impact it will have.

Vividness

Another vital element of effective imagery is vividness. Vividness means getting a very clear picture of what it looks like to perform well. Vivid images include sharp angles and colors as well as details like the lines on a tennis ball. Images that are big, bright, and captivating are more powerful than small, dim, and freeze-framed images. Be descriptive. Capture the moment.

The imagery script of the orange is a good example of vividness. You may want to go back and recall the orange exercise on page 106 and pay attention to the details of all the sensations related to the plump, juicy orange. Then, I invite you to try creating a lifelike image specific to your sport. Be creative and paint the scene in as much detail as possible. Look at the equipment, how is it unique? Think of the subtle sounds, sights, smells, tastes, movements, and moods that occur during training. Maybe you often hear geese fly by during training or you relish in seeing the brilliant green grass on the field and the invigorating scent. Take the time to delight in all of the sensory details you love about your sport.

After you progress to using imagery in training, the next step is to create a personalized imagery script for competition. While doing so, go through your pre-competition routine. Tune into all the sensations you usually feel during the build-up to competition. Imagine what you want your mental, emotional, and physical experience to be like. Be specific and descriptive. Really make those images come alive. Ultimately, you are savoring the feeling that everything is right, just as it should be. You are ready. You are confident. A helpful mantra I incorporate into a pre-competition imagery script is: *Breathe. Believe. Brave.*

Another way to help experience vivid images is to listen to or watch a video of your favorite performance. Then, close your eyes and recreate the images you see, feel, and hear. Watching videos of athletes you admire is another way to use imagery to spark inspiration, learn a new skill, and gain belief in your ability.

If vivid images are difficult for you, or the athletes you coach, then it is incredibly helpful for the beginner imager, and even veteran imagers, to use kinesthetic imagery. *Kinesthetic imagery* involves putting your body into the same position that you are trying to visualize or using equipment specific to the sport activity. For example, to help a kayaker visualize the Eskimo roll he or she would sit in a boat with a paddle in hand. Then, the kayaker imagines all the senses involved in rolling and slightly moves his or her body to facilitate a realistic visualization of the roll.

Kinesthetic imagery improves motor performance because the mechanism of kinesthetic imagery overlaps with brain areas (i.e., cerebellum, basal ganglia, premotor cortex) involved in overt motor performance (Ridderinkhof, & Brass, 2015). Consequently, the gymnast preparing for competition stands with her eyes closed next to the balance beam and begins to imagine her back tuck in her mind's eye. While dropping her arms to initiate the imagined back tuck, the gymnast is using kinesthetic imagery. Kinesthetic imagery lights up areas of the brain like the cerebellum (a small portion of the brain located where the spinal cord meets the brain and plays an important role in regulating fear and pleasure as well as fine-tuning motor activity) and the basal ganglia (at the base of the forebrain and responsible for procedural learning). When stimulated, these brain centers regulate voluntary motor movements (i.e., posture, balance, coordination) and coordinate smooth and balanced muscular activity. Lindsay Vonn, currently the most successful women's World Cup alpine skier of all time, practices a type of kinesthetic imagery where she uses the palms of her hands as if they were skies while she is visualizing the course before a competition.

Lastly, if you're anything like me and have a terrible time imagining even a simple image, then try the following kinesthetic imagery exercise. It's helped me and the athletes I work with to improve imagery ability.

Mental Exercise: Kinesthetic Imagery: An Instant Replay

Action Task: Stand tall with your feet together and arms relaxed at your side. Take in all the sights, sounds, tastes, and feelings around you. Slowly bend your right knee as high as you can with your right foot flexed. Notice your balance, any muscle tightness, and how you are talking to yourself. Slowly lower your right knee. Feel your foot gently touch the floor. While standing on two feet again, notice your balance. Begin to switch sides and slowly bend your left knee as high as you can with your left foot flexed. Notice any sensations you are experiencing. Slowly lower your knee so you're standing on 2 feet again.

Mental Task: While standing, imagine all the sights, sounds, tastes, and feelings around you. In your mind's eye, feel and see yourself slowly bending your right knee as you just did a moment ago. Begin to lower your right knee and feel your right foot touch the floor. Switch to your left side and imagine bending your left knee as high as you can. Lower your left knee back to a standing position while accounting for all your senses.

Discussion: How clear was your image? Could you feel your leg move? Including some physical movement with imagery can help to create a vivid scene. Given the physical nature of sports, using movements within the imagery script can help an athlete to create a more realistic mental scenarios. This optimizes the effectiveness of imagery and enhances self-awareness. A simple tool to gain greater self-awareness and evaluate imagery effectiveness can be found in Table 6.1. Table 6.1 is an imagery ability general assessment that can be used to evaluate progress as an athlete gradually improves imagery skills.

Controllability

Along with vividness, controllability is another characteristic of imagery. Controllability is the ability to manipulate the visual environment at will. It is the capacity to alter the shape of an image, change the color, as well as see and feel the image exactly as it should be. With controllability you can focus on and manipulate images. As you master controllability, you

Table 6.1 Imagery ability general assessment

	Rate how well you were able to...	Very poor				Very well
1.	...employ your senses	1	2	3	4	5
2.	...see vivid images	1	2	3	4	5
3.	...hear the sounds	1	2	3	4	5
4.	...evoke a taste	1	2	3	4	5
5.	...feel yourself move	1	2	3	4	5
6.	...attend to moods and emotions	1	2	3	4	5
7.	...control images	1	2	3	4	5

are able to navigate the images to accomplish what you want instead of seeing yourself make errors. The key to controllability is practice. You can practice controllability via navigating images through time and space by using the following mental exercise.

Mental Exercise: Controllability

Activity: After some slow, calming breaths, see three circles in your mind's eye. The first circle is black, the second circle is gray, and the third circle is white (see Figure 6.1). Get a sense of these shapes, their color, brightness, and their relationship to each other as well as the size and the space between them. There is more there than you ever realized. Close your eyes and keep this image in your head. Continue to breathe deeply and see each of the circles aligned horizontally. Think about the colors. Move the black circle to the lower left hand corner of your vision. Move the grey circle to the upper left hand corner. Move the white circle to the middle. Where is the black circle? The grey circle? The white circle? Shrink the white circle to half of its original size. Supersize the grey circle to twice its size. And change the black circle to a square. Change the white circle to red and the grey circle to blue.

Discussion:

1. Describe the picture.
2. On a scale of 1 to 10 (1 = low, 10 = high), rate your focus and your ability to move and manipulate the images.

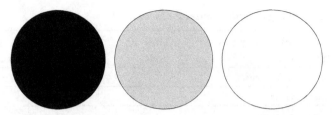

Figure 6.1 Controllability circles

By navigating your images, you experience what it's like to be focused as well as create and move images. To master controllability, first practice navigating simple images such as the three circles in Figure 6.1. Then, start working on sport-specific skills, such as developing technical skills, maintaining a positive attitude, or recalling defensive plays.

In controllability, it's also important to carefully rehearse what you want to happen and how you want to react in certain situations. For example, you can think about how your technique is neat, clean, and strong or feeling the power and ease of a difficult movement.

Without strong imagery control, athletes may find themselves making mistakes during imagery. For example, a softball player may unintentionally choke while imaging herself up to bat or a hockey player might visualize making a critical error and losing a game winning point. In the beginning, it's normal to imagine some negative images or thoughts during an imagery session. If you happen to imagine errors or hurtful thoughts, simply imagine coping effectively. Give yourself self-supporting images, feedback, or statements rather than self-pressuring instructions (Hardy & Oliver, 2014).

Self-supporting images and information (e.g., "You got this" or "Everyone makes mistakes") promote positivity, competence, and empowerment, which improves imagery and performance. On the contrary, *self-pressuring* is being overly critical and beating yourself up for a mistake (e.g., "You're so stupid" or "You messed up again"), which undermines skills and strengths and negatively impacts engagement, emotions, and the images necessary to perform to potential. Thus, it's important to remember that when you practice controllability, simply keep creating positive images with openness and nonjudgment.

Perspective

Recall the bedroom imagery script from the beginning of this section. Do you remember what perspective you took? Did you see and feel things as if a camera were on your head (i.e., as if you were looking through your own eyes)? Maybe you saw images as if you were an observer watching a movie or maybe it was a little of both perspectives. Answering these questions about perspective can inform you about your dominant visual sense. Seeing images as if you had a camera on your head, or through your own eyes, and actually feeling the imagined movements is known as an *internal imagery perspective*. If you viewed yourself from an outside observer as if you were sitting on the couch watching a movie of yourself, then this is an *external imagery perspective*.

One perspective is not better than the other. In fact, both internal and external imagery perspectives are effective for different reasons (Hale, 1994; Spittle & Morris, 2007). For example, an internal imagery perspective (i.e., seeing through your own eyes) gives individuals a greater kinesthetic feel (i.e., sensing the movement) than if they were using an external imagery perspective (i.e., watching a movie of yourself). Recent brain imaging research demonstrates this. In a study by Callow et al. (2016), the use of internal perspective imagery in combination with kinesthetic imagery (i.e., putting your body in the position of the activity you are imagining) activated more areas of the brain and lead to quicker driving times through a simulated slalom course compared to the imagery perspective alone. Thus, internal imagery perspective is typically better suited when athletes require a greater kinesthetic feel, such as a hockey goalie preparing to respond to a shot to the goal and he visualizes himself saving the dive and save the puck.

External imagery perspective can be effective in evaluating and refining form because an external perspective allows us to see the big picture. In sports where form and skill is fundamental (figure skating, dancing), seeing yourself rehearse detailed moves from an outside view can allow you to see your entire body move in space and evaluate how different body parts are moving in relation to each other (Hardy & Callow, 1999). In addition, replaying a past peak performance as if you were watching the highlights on TV can aid in confidence, composure, and motivation for future training and competitions.

In summary, both internal and external imagery perspectives improve performance. Athletes even report that they switch back and forth between both perspectives (Burton & Raedke, 2008). The best perspective is the one that helps athletes create the clearest and most vivid images possible.

Timing

Imagining a skill in *real time* is another key ingredient to imagery. Timing of an imagined skill should equally match that of the actual physical performance (Holmes & Collins, 2001; Wakefield et al., 2013). For example, an alpine skiing coach I was working with in Utah had one if his elite ski racers imagine decreasing his race time to achieve a personal record on a giant slalom course, a technical event in alpine skiing where athletes ski between 50 or more gates with about 1,000-foot vertical drop in the course. Each day before practice the ski coach timed the athlete's imagery script. Within a couple of weeks of practice, the athlete was able to imagine racing the giant slalom course in a time frame equal to his goal

A giant slalom skier uses imagery to better understand where the body and mind needs to be for a near seamless performance

race time. Later that season in competition, the athlete finished the course in the exact time he had imagined.

Practice

Mental imagery skills can only be improved through practice. The *first step* is helping athletes become invested. To grab an athlete's attention, I introduce imagery with the *orange slice* or *bolt on a string* mental exercise, both were featured at the beginning of this chapter. These are useful activities that help athletes value the power of imagery. Another way to spark interest is through reading testimonials from respected athletes who use imagery as a tool to improve performance, such as some of the quotes used in this chapter.

After an athlete practices imagery skills, the *second step* is to assess an athlete's ability to create vivid, controlled, and lifelike images. Measuring imagery ability involves determining an athlete's ability to produce imagery content, not necessarily determining the underlying reason for using imagery (Williams & Cumming, 2011). For example, two trail runners may imagine performing proper technique for running downhill. One runner may use this image to improve running technique while the same image may be used by the second runner to enhance confidence. Consequently, images serve many functions. As a result, many researchers measure imagery ability based on one's ability to produce an image. Yet, as psychology researcher Allen Paivio (1985) states, "[t]here is no single best measure [when assessing imagery ability] and the trick is to find [a method] that is most directly related to the specific task under consideration" (p. 27S).

Two examples of methods used to assess imagery ability that are also included in this chapter are: *the imagery ability general assessment* and *the sport imagery ability questionnaire.*

For a quick, general method to gauge an athlete's strengths and weaknesses in generating an image, they can complete the imagery ability general assessment found in Table 6.1 on page 127. This seven-question assessment is not validated through research, but it can be used as a quick field assessment tool to get a sense of imagery ability. To incorporate this imagery assessment tool, first select an imagery script of your choice, such as the bedroom imagery, instant replay, or a personalized imagery script. Second, go through the imagery. After completing the imagery, have athletes rate how well they were able to create and control the images by completing Table 6.1. Finally, discuss the results, highlight strengths, and target areas of improvement. The imagery ability general assessment can be used as a one-time assessment or as a means to evaluate progress overtime as an athlete gradually improves imagery skills.

For a comprehensive, valid, and reliable instrument to measure an athlete's ability to generate images of their sport experiences, one can use the Sport Imagery Ability Questionnaire (SIAQ; Williams & Cumming, 2011, 2014). The SIAQ is designed to measure the ability to imagine different content that an athlete would often use within the context of their sport (i.e., skills, strategies, goals, emotions, and mastering difficult events). It is an effective tool for both research and applied purposes because it provides the practitioner as well as the athlete with information regarding current imaging capacities. It also helps individuals better understand the content they may find easier or more difficult to visualize. The SIAQ is 15 questions and can be used as either a one-time assessment or gauge how imagery ability changes over time.

Sport Imagery Ability Questionnaire (SIAQ)

Instructions:
The purpose of this questionnaire is to obtain information about your ability to generate a number of sport and performance-related images.

For each item, bring the requested image to your mind. Do this with your eyes CLOSED. Then rate how easy it was to form this image (1 = very hard, 4 = not easy or hard, 7 = very easy). Circle the appropriate rating based on the scale provided. For example, some athletes may find imaging themselves kicking a football neither easy nor hard and therefore select 4.

Please be as accurate as possible and take as long as you feel necessary to arrive at the proper rating for each image. There are no right or wrong answers.

In relation to my sport, how easy is it for me to image...	Very hard to image	Hard to image	Somewhat hard to image	Neutral (not easy or hard)	Somewhat easy to image	Easy to image	Very easy to image
1. Making new plans or strategies in my head	1	2	3	4	5	6	7
2. Giving 100 percent effort even when things are not going well	1	2	3	4	5	6	7
3. Refining a particular skill	1	2	3	4	5	6	7
4. The positive emotions I feel while doing my sport	1	2	3	4	5	6	7
5. Myself winning a medal	1	2	3	4	5	6	7
6. Alternative plan or strategies	1	2	3	4	5	6	7
7. The anticipation and excitement associated with my sport	1	2	3	4	5	6	7
8. Improving a particular skill	1	2	3	4	5	6	7
9. Being interviewed as a champion	1	2	3	4	5	6	7
10. Staying positive after a setback	1	2	3	4	5	6	7
11. Making corrections to physical skills	1	2	3	4	5	6	7
12. Creating a new event or game plan	1	2	3	4	5	6	7
13. Myself winning	1	2	3	4	5	6	7
14. Remaining confident in a difficult situation	1	2	3	4	5	6	7

Scoring:
SIAQ can be scored in two different ways:

1. Global measure of sport imagery ability:
   All 15 items are averaged to produce one score reflective of sports imagery. Add the score for all 15 items and divide this value by 15.
2. Separate subscales of imagery ability:
   Items are averaged to form five separate subscales as follows:
   Skill imagery ability = (Item 3 + Item 8 + Item 12) ÷ 3
   Strategy imagery ability = (Item 1 + Item 6 + Item 13) ÷ 3
   Goal imagery ability = (Item 5 + Item 9 + Item 14) ÷ 3
   Affect imagery ability = (Item 4 + Item 7 + Item 11) ÷ 3
   Mastery imagery ability = (Item 2 + Item 10 + Item 15) ÷ 3

Adapted from Williams, S. E., & Cumming, J. (2011). Measuring athlete imagery ability: The sport imagery ability questionnaire. *Journal of Sport and Exercise Psychology, 33*, 416–440, by permission from Williams.

After measuring an athlete's imagery ability, the *third step* is learning how to improve these skills. In the beginning stages of imagery, practice sessions should only be a few minutes each day. The experience should be fun and user friendly. Initially practice should take place in a quiet environment. Introductory sessions should begin by visualizing objects (i.e., the orange or circles) or a safe place (i.e., bedroom, mountain stream) and the athlete should try to capture a moment and create clear, bright, and vivid images. More advanced imagers can then begin to manipulate the images; for example, peeling the orange or moving the circles. The key is to first learn how to create and recreate simple mental images, then, lengthen the time and complexity of the imagery session.

The *fourth step* is to apply imagery to sport-specific scenarios. There are countless ways to use imagery during training. For example, for a few minutes before training, an athlete can imagine what they want to experience or accomplish during the day's session. A sample of a short imagery script for a hard training day could include the following:

Mental Exercise: Pre-training Imagery Script

In a seated or lying position and with good posture, connect with your inhale and exhale. Simply take a moment to relax before mentally preparing for practice. Inhale deeply. Exhale completely. On your next inhale, slowly start to imagine the beginning of warm ups. Despite however your day has gone, imagine feeling strong and ready to tackle today's training. You are excited to practice and even more thrilled that you will learn something new. You feel fit, strong, and poised. You know that you are well prepared for anything that comes your way. Notice the confidence rising inside of you. As you transition from warm ups to training, you are self-assured because you've conquered this terrain before. You are ready. When training gets tough, you embrace the challenge because you know that nothing worthwhile is ever easy. During the toughest part of training you continually go above and beyond your expectations. As the training session comes to an end, take a moment to notice the pride you experience in knowing that you've tried your best. You improved today. With this self-acknowledgment, you feel victorious! Before opening your eyes, take a moment to set an intrinsically motivating goal to achieve today. Now see yourself accomplishing this goal. Take one deep breath. Open your eyes when you are ready. Now, have a great practice. The end.

The goal during this phase of imagery skill development is to introduce applying imagery to sport and encouraging athletes to practice imagery on their own as part of their daily routine. Sport-specific imagery is meant to evoke a positive sensory experience that empowers athletes to enjoy and embrace the pursuit of excellence, as a player and as a person. It teaches athletes how to set a positive frame of mind for living and performing.

Practicing imagery only a few minutes a day can sharpen an athlete's skills (Burton & Raedeke, 2008). In the beginning, keeping imagery short and fun can encourage athletes to practice on their own. For example, here's a quick imagery script that helps me to remember the pure joy in my beloved sport of skiing. *Imagine the kind of run that make skiers giggle in glee as they descend through a billowing cloud of their own soft powder... and emerge at the bottom coated in white frosting. It's fun to unleash your power through play.* This 10-second imagery helps me to remember the enjoyment and satisfaction that skiing brings to me.

Imagery is meant to evoke a positive sensory experience that empowers athletes to enjoy and embrace the pursuit of excellence as well as teach athletes how to set a positive frame of mind for living and performing. (PC: Mike Leake)

Another way to apply imagery in training is through teaching athletes to visualize proper form before doing a technical skill. When using imagery for *sport-specific skills*, it's important to remember to start with simple sport skills and build up to more complex techniques as athletes become more competent in their use of imagery.

To help an athlete use imagery for skill development, first encourage them to form an image of the skill they are about to execute. Second, have them practice forming the image with as much detail as possible until it is firmly etched into their neural filing cabinet. Then, have the athlete try to kinesthetically feel the skill as they imagine it. Finally, physically execute the skill. As Master swordsmans Yagū Munernori (1571–1646) said, "See first with your mind, then with your eyes, and finally with your body."

Other ways you can help athletes develop effective images are by using cues to activate all the senses, incorporating sports equipment as props, focusing on the meaning and significance of the image, or doing a simple kinesthetic movement as part of the imagery practice. Vivid cues, like peeling a Band-Aid off your shoe to create the appropriate foot gait in running, triggers a clear image of the proper form one is trying to achieve. Some athletes find it helpful to use a prop or object to focus, such as a photograph of a big mountain ski competition to imagine oneself skiing a specific line in the course. Finding meaning to your image sparks pleasure and, consequently, motivation and empowerment to reach your potential. Many athletes also find that simple movements (i.e., golfer moving their arms like a pendulum) makes it easier to create bright, clear, and vivid images.

The *last step* to mastering the skill of imagery is to incorporate it into competition. It is essential that athletes and coaches recognize that imagery is a skill and must be practiced consistently before use in competition. Athletes can use imagery the night before a competition, in the locker room before a game, during breaks in action or after a competition. For example, after finishing eighth in the 2006 Olympics, the day after a serious crash, Lindsey Vonn speaks to the power of imagery,

> *Before I skied again, I visualized the course about 20 times, like I was skiing it. I could see every bump, every jump. That helped me concentrate on exactly what I had to do. I wasn't surprised to finish. I would have been surprised to crash again.*

One way to help transition imagery from practice to competition is to create a race simulation imagery script. Initially, the race simulation imagery session should be kept short, about 5 minutes depending on the age and attention span of the athlete. As athletes practice, the race simulation imagery time can be lengthened to 10 to 15 minutes. Within the script, possibly include the venue and competition details such as the start of the race, a specific tactic, or a required skill or movement. As an example, I created a sample imagery script for a cross country skier that is included at the end of this chapter.

One last idea to incorporate imagery into practice and competition, *imagine the strength of your spirit animal* (i.e., ermine, wolf, river otter, eagle). Imagine your spirit animal charging through the workout or easily and effortlessly competing despite feeling fatigued. This may sound cheesy; however, I invite you to try it. For example, in 2014, an ultra-runner client of mine began to imagine her spirit animal, a wolverine, in training. She used this same imagery, as well as a few other mental tools (i.e., pace don't race, 1 minute to wallow), as she raced to an amazing second place in The Bear, a grueling 100-mile endurance run, even beating the coach that physically trained her.

Tim Ferris's (2017) new book, *Tools for Titans*, also introduces the concept of using spirit animals to achieve optimal performance. Ferris created a 673-page book full of practical tips, tools, and routines of thousands of world-class performers around the globe. There was one question he asked all these athletes, artists, billionaires, and icons that sparked an emotional charge, "What's your spirit animal?"

In summary, to achieve maximum benefits from imagery, it's critical that athletes have a consistent, systematic practice integrated into their training and competition routine. I've repeatedly drilled this point because athletes often miss the mark on this. They mistakenly use imagery the day of a competition as a magic solution, but rarely practice it in training. The more you deliberately practice, the better and more effective you become in imagining new sports skills, refining technique, building confidence, developing attention, and visualizing success. This is backed by evidence (Robin et al., 2007; Munroe-Chandler et al., 2012; Vealey & Greenleaf, 2001). Although the effectiveness of imagery increases for those reporting a higher ability to create an image, this ability can be developed through investment of time and effort (Hall, 2001). The goal: help athletes find value in practicing imagery and help them build effective imagery skills into their daily practice and competition routines.

Simplicity Is Supreme

This chapter decoded the elements of imagery. This decoding was meant to provide tools to effectively create a personalized imagery script. There was a lot of information presented in this chapter. Hopefully you are not overwhelmed by the prospect of using this powerful performance enhancing tool. In an attempt to keep it simple and straightforward (KISS), consider the aim of imagery: *see it, experience it, and enjoy it* (SEE).

Here are three critical components to successfully practice imagery:

1. Vividly *see* yourself performing optimally (S).
2. Deeply *experience* yourself performing competently (E).
3. Sincerely *enjoy* yourself in the moment (E).

Summary

- Imagery is using all the senses to create or recreate experiences in the mind.
- When using imagery, your brain creates a mental blueprint of your movements. By visualizing something you are ingraining and strengthening that specific movement blueprint and it becomes more automatic as it is ingrained into muscle memory. This reduces the chance of performing an error when the movement is actually performed.
- Images that have meaning have more depth and, thus, a greater potential impact on performance.
- The most powerful factor that influences the effectiveness of imagery is consistent use and practice of the imagery skill, meaning, the more one practices imagery the more likely it is to enhance performance.
- The seven hallmarks of an effective imagery script are: energy management multisensory, vividness, controllability, timing, perspective, and practice.
- When beginning to learn imagery skills, an athlete should manage their energy by remaining relaxed. An athlete progresses energy management skills during imagery by matching their individual zone of functioning needed to execute a skill or prepare for a best attempt to their image. This activates the appropriate physiological responses (i.e., increased heart rate, increased focus) to perform optimally.
- Multisensory is another characteristic of imagery ability. Multisensory is activating all your senses, moods, and meanings attached to the image to create a lifelike scene.

- Another important element of imagery is vividness. Vividness is creating a clear, bright and lifelike picture of a successful performance.
- Controllability refers to forming, maintaining and trans- forming images at will. By practicing controllability you are navigating the images as desired.
- Timing in imagery should match that of the physical perfor- mance.
- Both internal and external imagery perspectives are effective vantage points. Each perspective has unique advantages. Internal imagery perspective is typically better suited when athletes require a greater kinesthetic feel. For example, when a hockey goalie is preparing to respond to a shot to the goal and he visualizes himself time the dive to save the puck. External imagery can be effective in evaluating and refining form, such as when gymnasts want to see their entire body move through space. While athletes can practice using both perspectives, it's important that they use the perspective that produces the most vivid and lifelike images.
- Practice is required to develop imagery ability (i.e., develop all of their senses in their imagery, use vivid cues, practice partial movements) and efficacy. After athletes practice on a consis- tent basis, they can build imagery into their daily practice and competition routines.
- Assessment of imagery ability is to gauge an athlete's strengths, weaknesses, and ease of generating an image. Instruments to assess imagery ability include the imagery ability general assessment and the SIAQ.
- The overall aim of imagery practice is to *see* yourself perform- ing your best; *experience,* and capture the full moment and *enjoy* the sensory experience.

Seeing Is Believing: Cross Country Imagery Script

Begin by closing your eyes and use a technique to relax your body and your mind.

As you arrive to the venue, you notice that the sky is blue and there is a gentle breeze on your face. You smell the crispness of an early morning. The sun is just peaking over the ridge for the first time today. You feel its warmth on your back as you walk over to pick up your race packet. The excitement in the air is undeniable as you observe the other racers and event coordinators. The thrill of racing is exhilarating and it reminds you of why you love to compete in these events. As you set out for your warm up, you hear the cold, dry snow squeak under your ski boots with each step. As you put each pole strap on, the Velcro makes a familiar RIP, RIP. You bend down to clip each boot into the bindings, SNAP, SNAP. As you start your warm up, you feel the track is firm and your skis are fast. You are reminded of your best race; you felt a similar ease during that warm up. Your legs feel relaxed, yet powerful as you effortlessly stride up the first steep hill. You remind yourself of the cue word LIGHT and you feel a vibrant energy surrounding you and energizing you as you begin to reach the top of the hill. Enjoy this free-flowing, healthy energy sweeping through your body. Your triceps and back feel strong as you crest the hill and the grade levels out. This builds your confidence for the remainder of the warm up.

The race is about to begin. As you are stripping off your warm-up jacket and pants at the start line, you KNOW everything is in place for a great race. Your skis, your training, even your breakfast have settled well. You've gone over your last minute details in your head and you know this will be your best race. You're well prepared for this event and you are feeling mentally strong. Your body remembers how to ski and how to ski well. Take a few deep, slow breaths, and savor this feeling. Everything is right, just as it should be. You are ready.

The race official calls your event. Imagine yourself at the starting line. What do you see, feel, hear, and smell around you? The official commands "On your mark." You bend down into your starting position. At the sound of the gun, you take off with a powerful push onto the snow. Your technique is neat, clean, and strong. You feel the power and ease of your stride. As you glide, you feel your arms and leg in complete synchrony. You hear yourself breathe, heavy, yet controlled. With each push you feel stronger and stronger, moving across the snow with speed. You notice all the other racers around you but no one encroaches into your space. You made it out of the fray of the start and now strive to race your own race. You concentrate on your technique and pacing.

You're coming around for the second half of the race. Attack the second half. You remind yourself of the cue word LIGHT and you feel a vibrant energy surrounding you as you begin to reach the top of a hill. You push yourself above and beyond your expectations. You feel physically powerful as you begin to double pole as the grade levels out. This strength builds your confidence, you feel quick and powerful as the race continues.

As you approach the finish, you are still feeling very energized. You've trained for this race and it feels great. You use your strong arms and powerful legs to propel yourself forward. With 200 meters to go, you kick into overdrive. Faster, stronger, better. As you pull toward the finish you feel your speed increasing. You are completely focused on pushing toward the finish. You are doing everything as it should be done, with poise and with purpose. With each push you dig into your reserves. Pushing, propelling, and surging forward until you cross the finish line.

You begin to regain awareness of everything around you, colors come into focus, and you hear the crowd. You realize you've achieved your goal. You become aware of the feelings of excitement and accomplishment. Pride builds inside you. You have succeeded. You are a great skier.

References

Ahsen, A. (1984). ISM: The Triple Code Model for Imagery and Psychophysiology. *Journal of mental imagery*.

Burton, D., & Raedeke, T. D. (2008). Imagery. In *Sport Psychology for Coaches* (pp. 67–82). Champaign, IL: Human Kinetics.

Callow, N., Jiang, D., Roberts, R., & Edwards, M. G. (2016). Kinesthetic Imagery Provides Additive Benefits to Internal Visual Imagery on Slalom Task Performance. *Journal of Sport and Exercise Psychology*, 1–18.

Carpenter, W.B. (1984). *Principles of mental physiology*. New York: Appleton.

Cumming, J., & Hall, C. (2002). Deliberate imagery practice: the development of imagery skills in competitive athletes. *Journal of Sports Sciences*, *20*(2), 137–145.

Cumming, J., & Ramsey, R. (2009). Sport imagery interventions. In S. Mellalieu & S. Hanton (eds.), *Advances in applied sport psychology: A review* (pp. 5–36). London: Routledge.

Ferris, T. (2017). *Tools of titans: The tactics, routines, and habits of billionaires, icons, and world-class performers.* New York: Houghton Mifflin Harcourt.

Hale, B. D. (1994). Imagery perspectives and learning in sports performance. *Imagery in sports and physical performance. Farmingdale: Baywood,* 75–96.

Hall, C. R. (2001). Imagery in sport and exercise. In R. N. Singer, H. A. Hausenblas, & C. M. Janelle (eds.), *The handbook of sport psychology* (2nd ed., pp. 529–549). New York: John Wiley & Sons Inc.

Hardy, J., & Oliver, E. J. (2014). *Self-talk, positive thinking, and thought stopping.* Thousands Oaks, CA: Sage.

Hardy, L., & Callow, N. (1999). Efficacy of external and internal visual imagery perspectives for the enhancement of performance on tasks in which form is important. *Journal of Sport and Exercise Psychology, 21*(2), 95–112.

Hird, J. S., Landers, D. M., Thomas, J. R., & Horan, J. J. (1991). Physical practice is superior to mental practice in enhancing cognitive and motor task performance. *Journal of Sport and Exercise Psychology, 13*(3), 281–293.

Holmes, P. S., & Collins, D. J. (2001). The PETTLEP approach to motor imagery: A functional equivalence model for sport psychologists. *Journal of Applied Sport Psychology, 13*(1), 60–83.

Kabat-Zinn, J., Wheeler, E., Light, T., Skillings, A., Scharf, M. J., Cropley, T. G., & Bernhard, J. D. (1998). Influence of a mindfulness meditation-based stress reduction intervention on rates of skin clearing in patients with moderate to severe psoriasis undergoing photo therapy (UVB) and photochemotherapy (PUVA). *Psychosomatic Medicine, 60*(5), 625–632.

King, K. (2010). A review of the effects of guided imagery on cancer patients with pain. *Complementary Health Practice Review, 15*(2), 98–107.

Kumar, A. M. (2015). An outcome of periodized small side games with and without mental imagery on playing ability among intercollegiate level soccer players. *Indian Journal of Science and Technology, 8*(36).

Lang, P. J. (1979). A bio-informational theory of emotional imagery. *Psychophysiology, 16*(6), 495–512.

MacIntyre, T. E., Moran, A. P., Collet, C., & Guillot, A. (2013). An emerging paradigm: A strength-based approach to exploring mental imagery. *Mental Imagery, 39.*

Martin, K. A., Moritz, S. E., & Hall, C. R. (1999). Imagery use in sport: A literature review and applied model. *The sport psychologist, 13*(3), 245–268.

Munroe-Chandler, K. J., Hall, C. R., Fishburne, G. J., Murphy, L., & Hall, N. D. (2012). Effects of a cognitive specific imagery intervention on the soccer skill performance of young athletes: Age group comparisons. *Psychology of Sport and Exercise, 13*(3), 324–331.

Murphy, S., Jowdy, D., & Durtschi, S. (1990). Report on the US Olympic Committee survey on imagery use in sport. Colorado Springs, CO: US Olympic Training Center.

Murphy, S., Nordin, S. M., & Cumming, J. (2008). Imagery in sport, exercise and dance. In T. Horn (ed.), *Advances in sport and exercise psychology* (3rd ed., pp. 297–324). Champaign, IL: Human Kinetics.

Nicklaus, J. (1974). Golf my way. New York: Heinemann.

Orlick, T., & Partington, J. (1988). Mental links to excellence. *The sport psychologist, 2*(2), 105-130.

Paivio, A. (1985). Cognitive and motivational functions of imagery in human performance. *Canadian Journal of Applied Sport Sciences, 10*, 22S–28S.

Parnabas, V., Parnabas, J., & Parnabas, A. M. (2015). The influence of mental imagery techniques on sport performance among hockey players. *International Journal of Physical and Social Sciences, 5*(4), 217.

Ridderinkhof, K. R., & Brass, M. (2015). How Kinesthetic Motor Imagery works: a predictive-processing theory of visualization in sports and motor expertise. *Journal of Physiology-Paris, 109*(1), 53–63.

Robin, N., Dominique, L., Toussaint, L., Blandin, Y., Guillot, A., & Le Her, M. (2007). Effect of motor imagery training on service return accuracy in tennis: The role of imagery ability. *International Journal of Sport and Exercise Psychology, 2*, 175–186.

Sackett, R. S. (1934). The influences of symbolic rehearsal upon the retention of a maze habit. *Journal of General Psychology, 13*, 113–128.

Spittle, M., & Morris, T. (2007). Internal and external imagery perspective measurement and use in imagining open and closed sports skills: An exploratory study. *Perceptual and Motor Skills, 104*(2), 387–404.

Vealey, R. S., & Greenleaf, C. A. (2001). Seeing is believing: Understanding and using imagery in sport. *Applied sport psychology: Personal growth to peak performance, 4*, 247–272.

Wakefield, C., Smith, D., Moran, A. P., & Holmes, P. (2013). Functional equivalence or behavioural matching? A critical reflection on 15 years of research using the PETTLEP model of motor imagery. *International Review of Sport and Exercise Psychology, 6*(1), 105–121.

Williams, S. E., & Cumming, J. (2014). *The Sport Imagery Ability Questionnaire Manual*. Birmingham, UK: Author. doi:10.13140/RG.2.1.1608.6565

Williams, S. E., & Cummings, J. (2011). Measuring athlete imagery ability: The sport imagery ability questionnaire. *Journal of Sport and Exercise Psychology, 33*, 416–440.

About the Authors

Christina Heilman, PhD, ATC, CSCS, is a coach, author, researcher, and speaker in the applied field of mental training and excellence. Christina finds her personal pursuit of excellence with powder skiing, rock climbing, and trail running in the mountains. From her own experiences as an athlete and high-achiever, Christina knows what it feels like to endure pressure, navigate fear, overcome self-doubt, maintain confidence, and preserve inner joy to maximize one's potential. She believes that the skills that help someone be the best they can be in sports are the same ones that will help them in other parts of their life.

It's really Christina's diverse experiences, academic degrees, and achievements in both the mind and body that has helped her coach hundreds of youth, recreational, collegiate, and professional athletes and coaches to achieve healthy, long-lasting habits in reaching peak levels of performance without destroying their health and well-being in the process.

In 2012, the Association of Applied Sport Psychology awarded Christina the Dissertation of the Year Award for her pioneering research in the areas of motivation, achievement, and positive development through sport. She is also double board-certified as an Athletic Trainer (ATC) and Strength and Conditioning Coach (CSCS). In addition, Christina has an extensive history of professional activity including: international conference presentations, publications in peer-reviewed journals, teaching in universities, innovative programming for youth to develop positive mental skills for sports and life, and development of cutting-edge tools for elite mountain athletes to optimize health and performance.

Chris lives in Driggs, Idaho with her husband, son, and her passion for learning new things. Visit her website at www.mindset-coach.com.

Index

OTHER TITLES IN OUR HEALTH, WELLNESS, AND EXERCISE SCIENCE COLLECTION

Abigail Larson, Southern Utah University, *Editor*

Injury Recognition and Prevention: Lower and Upper Extremity
by Genevieve Ludwig and Megan Streveler

Fuel for Sport: The Basics
by Abigail J. Larson

*Sports Nutrition Strategies for Success: A Practical Guide to
Improving Performance Through Nutrition*
by Abigail J. Larson and Kary Woodruff

Introduction to General Medical Conditions
by Genevieve Ludwig and Megan Streveler-Lundstrom

Momentum Press is one of the leading book publishers in the field of engineering, mathematics, health, and applied sciences. Momentum Press offers over 30 collections, including Aerospace, Biomedical, Civil, Environmental, Nanomaterials, Geotechnical, and many others.

Momentum Press is actively seeking collection editors as well as authors. For more information about becoming an MP author or collection editor, please visit http://www.momentumpress.net/contact

---

Announcing Digital Content Crafted by Librarians

Momentum Press offers digital content as authoritative treatments of advanced engineering topics by leaders in their field. Hosted on ebrary, MP provides practitioners, researchers, faculty, and students in engineering, science, and industry with innovative electronic content in sensors and controls engineering, advanced energy engineering, manufacturing, and materials science.

Momentum Press offers library-friendly terms:

- perpetual access for a one-time fee
- no subscriptions or access fees required
- unlimited concurrent usage permitted
- downloadable PDFs provided
- free MARC records included
- free trials

The **Momentum Press** digital library is very affordable, with no obligation to buy in future years.

For more information, please visit **www.momentumpress.net/library** or to set up a trial in the US, please contact **mpsales@globalepress.com.**

CPSIA information can be obtained
at www.ICGtesting.com
Printed in the USA
LVHW031508240919
632125LV00011B/1194/P